Acts of Holy Spirit Through A Regular Guy

Reporting God's Power
To The Next Generation

By L. F. Low

Zoë*Life*
Publishing

Zoë*Life*

Publishing
900 N League Road
Colfax, IA USA 50054

Printed in the United States of America on acid free
paper by Createspace.com

Copyright @ 2015
Cover designed by Andrew Spurlin /
Detroit Lakes, Minnesota, USA
Edited by Daryl Jung / Waverly, Iowa, USA

Low, L. F.
Acts of Holy Spirit Through
a Regular Guy /
By L. F. Low

ISBN-13:978-1519439017
ISBN-10:1519439016

1. Christian life, 2. Adventure, 3. Spirit life
I. Title
Set in Garamond

All rights reserved. No part of this book may be reproduced or transmitted in any form or by any means, electronic or mechanical, including photocopying, recording, or by any information storage and retrieval system, without permission in writing from the Publisher.

Table Of Contents

Dedication..iii

Forward iv

Prologue..1

Chapter 1..4

Death: The Beginning Of Life

Chapter 2..12

Preparation For The Trip Ahead

Chapter 3..24

Cleaning Up My Mess

Chapter 4..32

The Loser Wins

Chapter 5..40

Holy Spirit University

Chapter 6..52

The Name Above All Names

Chapter 7..63

For As We Think We Are

Chapter 8	Whatever You Ask In My Name	72
Chapter 9	South Of The Border	92
Chapter 10	Hungry For God	101
Chapter 11	Forgiven, Forgiven, Forgiven	109
Chapter 12	God Guides And Provides	125
Chapter 13	Holy Boldness For Battle	132
Chapter 14	If God Is For Us	141
Chapter 15	One More Year	161
Chapter 16	The Mask Lady	175

Chapter 17 183
Miracle In Houston
Epilogue 196

Dedication

I dedicate this book to my children and their children – all 16 of them – along with their spouses, and my great grandchildren.

Because of all the blessings I have received from the Lord, I believe it is my responsibility to report on the faithfulness and the power of God to the future generations.

Therefore I humbly present a few of my personal experiences – with the third Person of the Holy Trinity – in Acts of Holy Spirit Through a Regular Guy.

Love you forever;
Dad, Grandpa & Pastor Larry

Forward

"When did the miracles stop, Larry?"

As I read that question in this, my dear brother's book, Acts Of Holy Spirit Through A Regular Guy, my heart began to break.

This is probably one of the most common questions in our congregations today, and to be completely honest, it was one of my first questions as a new believer.

My idea of God came from my Catholic upbringing and the God that I heard about was always so distant – and nearly impossible to truly relate to or communicate with.

Thankfully, while I was a student at Teen Challenge of the Midlands, Brother Larry was there and he introduced me to the Holy Spirit.

Through this encounter with the Holy Spirit, in His perfect time, He explained to me the truth behind the lies that I once believed.

Brother Larry did what he does best; arranged the meeting for people to encounter the Holy Spirit. For nearly a year I had weekly meetings with Brother Larry as together we prayed, related and fellowshipped with the Holy Spirit.

I will never forget those meetings as they helped lay the foundation and revealed my calling to the nations.

This is a must read for any believer who is simply needing a reminder of how great our God really is and what He can do in anyone's life. As a direct result of Brother Larry's relationship with the Holy Spirit, my life is forever changed and now I am able to be a blessing to many throughout the nations.

Thank you Brother Larry for this incredible and humble book, which I pray will impact the lives of every reader.

Pastor Chris Buscher
Author of the My Confession series

All quotations from Scripture, unless otherwise noted, are from the New King James Version of The Holy Bible.

Prologue

Acts of Holy Spirit through a regular *guy*?
A presumptuous title, one might observe.
It may be for some. Not, certainly, from my perspective. Not now, anyway.

During my years of following God I have always felt that when in Heaven, we will all be able to view the Book of Acts as a movie, from each person's perspective, that has already unreeled during our journeys through life. Scriptures promise this to a degree.

Look at Psalm 56: 8-9.

"You number my wanderings; Put my tears into Your bottle; are they not in Your book?"

Not enough proof? Check Malachi 3:16.

"Then those who feared the Lord spoke to one another, And the Lord listened and heard them; So a

book of remembrance was written before Him for those who fear the Lord and who meditate on His name."

The Book of Acts is all about how the Holy Spirit worked through the Apostles Peter, Paul and ordinary folks like you and I to build and establish the Church. Because the Church is still being built, the book of Acts remains unfinished.

Every other book in the Bible has "amen" as its final word. Acts is the only exception. There is no amen simply because the book is still being written by those who still, and who will, submit to Him.

These final chapters of Acts will never be canonized (added to the Holy Bible), but will be just as Holy. They will be about the Holy Spirit still working, today, through His flesh and blood partners.

Everyone who dares to follow God will have their own chapter in the final Book of Acts – Acts of the Holy Spirit through… whoever *you* are.

I hope this book, my own chapter of Acts, will inspire readers to get as hungry for God as I am.

Herein is contained a catalogue of personal (often witnessed firsthand), rags-to-riches and death-to-life stories of real people. But it is not *about* them, or me. It is about my best friend, the amazing Holy Spirit.

It all started as this regular guy was working, trying to make a living and raise a family.

The story is so common it could have been easily totally ignored, but not by me. I want to shout from the mountain tops that God is *still* doing everything He did in the Book of Acts. He still searches for men and women who will submit to Him and dare to take that walk on the wild side.

The Holy Spirit is the star of this show, and the singular reason I can even record it.

The hero of these stories is none other than the Lord Jesus Christ.

Because of what He did well over 2000 years ago, we have access to the Holy Spirit and if we allow Him, He has access to us.

Simple.

These are not at all religious stories, either. Rather they are adventures in what can, and does, happen to regular folks who desire their own chapter in the final Book of Acts.

They are true tributes to some ordinary guys and gals who dared to take the courageous, adventurous route through life, trusting God all the way.

Chapter 1
Death: The Beginning Of Life

*I*t all began on an exceptionally bleak, blustering and sodden March morning in southern Iowa, as I dutifully trudged out to the barn for morning chores.

I had checked on the new lambs born just a day or two before; pulling the dead ones out of the shed and throwing them onto an ever-mounting pile atop the old tires I would later need to burn them.

That spring it rained almost every day. All I was waiting for was a couple of days reprieve from it, and a warm southerly breeze so I could ignite an inferno and watch my dreams and my future go up in smoke.

With each dead lamb and ewe added to the growing pile, my hopes of making it through another season shrank. Day after day the story was the same – more dead or dying sheep, even less hope.

Local veterinarians said they had never witnessed such a miserable year of widespread plague from the disease we had running rampant on our farm.

Considering the market value of the sheep, the cost of the daily feed bill and the vets who were trying to help me whip this thing, I was losing in excess of $20,000 a month. That may not seem like much now, but it was huge money in the late '70s.

I was sinking into a dark cesspool of despair with no hope of making my upcoming farm payment.

Failure was all I could see. My entire mind focused on a single dire thought – "You're a loser, fella," played continuously in my head.

Every time my wife went outside to check for new lambs, she would come back in tears. Every time I witnessed that my heart would break into a billion pieces, my spirit sinking even lower.

My wife's tears and sorrow of those days told me I was a colossal failure. I really had no other reason to keep on living if I couldn't even take care of my family. Even though she would never have said that, I read it in her actions and her pain; which was my grave misinterpretation of the experience.

Finally I could take it no longer. I decided to end our misery; after all, I "reasoned," I have enough life insurance (suicide clause be damned) to take care of my wife and three daughters – even pay off the farm should they decide to continue living there.

I was worth more dead than alive! Do you know how much it hurts to equate your value to economic conditions? It's humiliating beyond description!

I took the 20-guage shotgun out of our bedroom closet and loaded the chamber with one deer slug.

My plan was to crawl onto the pile of carcasses, put the shotgun barrel in my mouth and blow my head off; keeping all the mess outside easily disposed of with a few gallons of diesel fuel and a torch.

However, before going out to "solve" my problem, I thought I should measure the distance from the barrel to the trigger, making sure I could reach the trigger without ruining the position of the barrel. Everything had to be perfect; the gun barrel had to be pointing directly at the center of my brain-stem.

How embarrassing it would be to botch your final decision in life! Talk about confirming the feeling of being a total, over-the-top failure! I had to make sure I could physically do the job once I got there.

As I put the barrel in my mouth and reached with my right hand for the trigger, my jaw tightened as the taste of gun powder and oil touched the back part of my throat, making my gag reflex flex.

As if I had inhaled a giant lung-full of smelling salts, my eyes were opened instantly and I began to sob, realizing, for the first time that day, just what I was about to do.

The words of my paternal grandmother replayed in my head, "If you are ever in trouble, make sure you call on Jesus. He loves you and will help you."

It was her message every time I talked to her or received a letter or card, always the same – "Just call on Jesus."

As I look back on that now, I can see God's love for me and my grandma. She loved Jesus with all her heart and God was therefore able to speak through her, preparing me for this very moment.

I suddenly jumped to my feet with a sudden, clear understanding of just what I was about to do. I put the shotgun in the corner, and I cried out to Heaven.

"Jesus, if you are real I need some help right now! Grandma said You would help me. I don't want to die but right now I don't know how to live."

Suddenly my entire house was filled with a tangible, divine presence and, oddly enough, I suddenly found myself talking on the phone to a woman I had never met telling me Jesus' words in Matthew 6:33,

"But seek first the kingdom of God and His righteousness, and all these things shall be added to you."

How did she know I was having financial trouble? Who the heck is this person? I didn't even hear the phone ring. What on earth is going on here?

"Do we know each other? Why did you call me?" I asked.

She replied, "No, we have never met; I didn't know you were having trouble until you told me, and I didn't call you. You called me!"

How could I call someone I didn't know?

"In fact," I said, "I was just getting ready to end my troubles and now I am talking on the phone. How did you know to call me?"

She repeated herself, "I truly didn't. You called me, I assure you."

I suddenly felt very foolish and asked her to forgive my intrusion and then hurriedly hung up the phone.

I knew my wife and daughters would soon be returning from grocery shopping, so I rushed back to the bedroom to unload and put away the shotgun.

Still reeling from something that had completely escaped my understanding, I searched frantically. But I couldn't find it! I had to unload it and put it away so Dixie and the kids would never know what I had been planning!

Suddenly it came to me to look in the closet. And there it was! I pulled it out of the closet and opened the chamber to eject the shell; and to my surprise the gun was unloaded and, of all things, cleaned.

I checked the new box of shells and it was full just like it was when I took the shell out only a few minutes before.

"What the hell is going on here?" I said aloud.

The words, "You called on Jesus," came crashing instantly into my mind, so strongly they could have been audible through a loudspeaker.

My legs could no longer support me, my knees buckled and I went to the floor weeping, crying out in repentance for what I was preparing to do.

After a long period on the floor, saying over and over again I was sorry and explaining how miserable I felt my life had become, I suddenly sensed a calming, gentle touch on my back.

The words came once again to my head, "You are going to be alright, son. I love you. I don't want you to worry any longer. I will help you. I will take care of you if you let Me."

I got to my feet and somehow realized I was in the presence of God. I had never experienced anything like this in my 30 plus years of living.

I just seemed to *know* I was talking to Jesus. His words were not audible, but they impressed heavily on my mind. They seemed urgent. They penetrated my heart, bringing me hope, life and excitement for the future.

It was something I had never witnessed or experienced before – a sense of hope that I hadn't felt for quite some time at that point.

I knew I was in the presence of Royalty; my home was filled with His presence and my physical body tingled from head to foot. I didn't know it then, but the King of kings was in my home.

Crazy what a person thinks about at times like this. "Oh my God, I just said 'hell' and I was going out to kill myself! Is He here to end it for me? No, He said He would help take care of me.

"Oh, my God, what is going on?"

I continued to feel the incredibly soothing touch on my back. I was afraid to look up. But as I slowly opened my eyes and looked from side to side enough to see that there was no physical person with me, I still sensed His awesome presence within me.

I asked, "May I get up?" I immediately sensed Him say, "Of course you may."

I slowly got to my feet. Looking around, I pointed toward Heaven as I exclaimed, "I am very sorry to say this, but I don't know You! But I promise You this one thing: I am going to spend the rest of my life chasing after You until I get to know who You are.

"I want to know You, Jesus! I want to know You and to be with You!" I shuddered and sobbed.

But in a heartbeat I went from wanting to die to a desire to live so intense it frightened me, yet emboldened me.

In that same heartbeat the Name of Jesus took me from being a selfish heathen, who cared only about himself and the physical pleasures of life, to an intense hunger to help others find what I just found. And I wasn't even sure of what it was yet.

This was my first experience of being in His presence, teaching me how it felt. It would not, however, be the last or only time.

Thus began an adventure that would eventually change my life so completely that I currently struggle to even remember what life was once like before this experience – before I was born again.

It was the beginning of this regular guy's walk with God the Creator, Jesus Christ His Son, and the Holy Spirit; the best friend anyone could ever have.

Chapter 2
Preparation For Trip Ahead

"The journey of a thousand miles begins with a single step."
(Chinese philosopher Lao Tzu)

A few days later the weather changed dramatically. The sun popped through the grayness and burned away the heavy clouds that had completely covered Iowa since late January of that year.

It was a bright April day and the sun was warm, the sky was as blue as I had ever seen it, lightly dotted with huge cumulous clouds lazily floating overhead.

I was still overjoyed – and a bit stunned – from the amazing experience I had with Jesus just days before.

As I walked through the timber next to my house I looked up to Heaven and said rather emphatically, "Jesus please, don't let this stop! Pour it on, Lord. I don't know what you are doing; I have never experienced anything like this before and I like it. Please don't let it end. Please pour it on Lord, pour it on!

"Give me all you've got, Lord!"

At that same moment I felt the urge to sing praises to Him and the only song I knew that fit what I was feeling was my favorite, Amazing Grace.

As I lifted my voice to sing, my mind was thinking, "amazing grace, how sweet the sound that saved a wretch like me."

But what came out was quite different – a strange-sounding language that I had never heard before and that I certainly didn't understand. And I was singing it to the melody of Amazing Grace.

I stopped and shook my head and thought, "What just happened?"

I lifted my voice and tried it again. The same thing happened. A foreign-sounding language came spilling from my mouth. This time I went with it and continued to sing the melody, allowing the language to flow.

As I sang I began to feel like I was flying. I closed my eyes and lifted my hands toward Heaven and just worshiped Jesus with these strange-sounding words.

After a period of time, I can't remember exactly how long, I stopped singing and looked toward Heaven and attempted to ask, "What is going on, Lord?"

But again, these weird syllables cascaded wildly forth from my mouth.

By then, I couldn't speak in English! I remember feeling a little anxious with the idea that I had no control over the language that was issuing forth.

As my fear mounted, the thought came to me that whatever this was made me feel better than I had ever felt in my life. Absolutely astonishing!

I was a pretty heavy drinker in those days and never had alcohol made me feel *this* good.

At that same moment, I thought *I* was thinking, but now I know it was the Lord speaking to my mind.

"Open your Bible."

I went into the house and found the only Bible I had; an old Good News Bible I got from my Grandma's table after her death.

As I grabbed the Bible and sat down, the word "ax" came bounding into my mind. Confused, I looked (foolishly) in the index for the word "Ax."

After going through the Old Testament searching for "Ax" and finding nothing, I continued into the New Testament and quickly noticed there was no "Ax."

But there *was* an "Acts."

Well, it sounded like Ax. And it seemed right at that moment that I should read the Book of Acts.

"Dear Theophilus: In my first book I wrote about all the things that Jesus did and taught ..." (Acts 1:1)

I was stirred with excitement as I continued to read. I somehow knew I was going to find my answer to this strange occurrence that was happening to me.

Verse 8 said, "When the Holy Spirit comes upon you, you will be filled with power." And inside my head the Holy Spirit said, "That's what happened to you. Read on."

I was actually, palpably tingling as I continued to read.

Chapter 2:4 said, "They were all filled with the Holy Spirit and began to talk in other languages, as the Spirit enabled them to speak."

And again inside my head the Lord said, "That's what happened to you. Read on." And on and on I read with the same words being spoken to me as I read Acts 8:14-17, 10:45-46, 11:15-16, 19:6.

I read all 28 chapters of the Book of Acts that day with Holy Spirit as my Teacher, encouraging me to keep reading until I was confident that I had been baptized in the Holy Spirit.

As it says in Acts 11:16, I had been speaking in what the Bible calls "tongues."

It was a year or so later before I heard a preacher on the radio teaching baptism in the Holy Spirit.

During that teaching I realized that many others have had the same experience as I had. Yet a man didn't teach me. The Holy Spirit Himself taught me.

After that lesson I was able to speak in English once again. I was also able to go back to that strange tongue and speak it as I desired. Though I didn't fully understand it all then, it was a constant comfort to me and a continuous reminder of Jesus' presence.

* * *

This was a physically and emotionally horrible time for our family as we fought to clean up our financial mess.

We were losing our new home, due to an unrealistic surge in interest rates during the '80s; the recession in the city was devastation to the farmers.

Many farmers were losing everything they and the generations before them worked their lifetime to gain.

The infamous Willie Nelson began taking "Farm Aid" tours around the whole nation, raising money for and awareness about the families who once grew everyone's food but could no longer feed their own.

I continued to work in Des Moines during this time so, thank God, I was still able to feed mine.

One evening Dixie and the girls thought a night at home playing a board game called Life would be fun.

As I played with them I was gaining tokens and then I would lose them. I gained a house and as luck would have it, I lost it. I got so irritated and angry I threw the game pieces furiously into the air.

"I don't need this s^&%!" I practically screamed. "This is no game! This is torment! I'm living this crap every day; I don't need more torment than real life is already pouring on me right now!"

I stormed off to mix a drink and feel depressed, leaving my family in a state of fear and confusion.

I was so conflicted and confused in those days! I had just had one of the greatest experiences a man could ever have, and I knew intuitively that there was a great plan for my life. But I had no physical proof of anything of any magnitude happening.

I had just gotten fired from my job in town so I was trying my best to make a living selling light bulbs (which should have been turning on in my head!).

Dixie was right beside herself, trying desperately to encourage me. Yet she knew we were losing our new home and land while my young daughters had no clue why we were at odds with each other so much.

I was drinking heavily and the pressure we were under made me drink all the more.

But I had started reading the Bible again because of how I remembered it making me feel when I read through the Book of Acts.

Not knowing anything about the Bible, I started reading it like any normal book, left to right, top to bottom starting in Genesis 1:1, "In the beginning..."

I tried to read a chapter or two each day, sometimes during the day. As I literally waded my way through Genesis, Exodus, Leviticus, Numbers and, Deuteronomy, I wished I could proclaim that God was giving me tremendous revelations.

However, either He wasn't with me, or I was unable to receive Him. Very probably it was the latter.

I kept plugging along nevertheless, because I needed something that held a promise for me and I desperately needed the feeling I received the day I first read through the Book of Acts.

I invested in a new Bible sometime in this process, and I bought a New International Version because I liked the way it read and the salesman said it was the newest translation then available.

When I got to Isaiah 28 verse 11, the Lord spoke to me as I read,

"Very well then, with foreign lips and strange tongues God will speak to this people, to whom He said, 'This is the resting place, let the weary rest.'"

I suddenly remembered the feeling I had in the pasture speaking in that strange tongue. I remembered clearly how I felt as I continued to sing in that language. I felt refreshed and excited and it felt like I was soaring gracefully across the sky.

I looked toward Heaven and said, "God, is this for me? Is this why I felt so good in the timber?"

His response blew me right away. "Yes," He said. "This is for you. Enter in, son."

I began to speak in that strange language again and once again, I began to fly.

It was a year or two from then that I learned from the Book of Romans that this is allowing the Holy Spirit to pray for us, and through us, as we yield our tongue to Him (Romans 8:26, 27).

From that day on I made sure I allowed the Holy Spirit to pray for me, through me, every time I faced one of the many unpleasant aspects of losing everything that we were about to go through.

One day I was fed up with the situations I was facing in losing my home and I screamed, "This just isn't fair! I've worked hard for this Lord! This just isn't fair!"

As I wept, I sensed the Lord saying, "Just let go of it, son. I have so much more for you. Just let it go for Me and allow the opportunity for Me to show you."

I knew, somehow, He wanted me to quit fighting to save my worldly things and to just let them go. But the thought of it created within me more conflicts.

I wanted to let it go so I could just move on, but the thought of it made me sick as I thought of dealing with my family who was counting on me to save ourselves and everything we'd worked for.

To say the least, I was miserable being so elated with what God was showing me and so physically sick about how to communicate this to a wife who had not yet met the Master.

I was excited about God, but at the same time was so angry with Him for what I was going through.

I would tell Him how much I loved Him and appreciated Him in one breath and find myself cursing Him the next.

We were in such emotional pain in those days and I know now that it was God who helped us get through it all.

My drinking became heavier and more frequent as I struggled to understand what was going on.

Prior to this, everything I touched turned to gold. But here I was with everything I touched dying and the Federal Land Bank pressing me for a payment.

The day I found out I was not going to be able to save my home I was heading in to the Federal Land Bank to make my $20,000 annual payment.

I wrote the check and gave it to the clerk. He stamped it and filed it in his drawer and then he said, "That's not going to cover it."

"What did you say?" I asked incredulously and desperately.

"That's not going to cut it," he repeated.

"What do you mean, that's not going to cover it?" I snapped back viciously.

Instantly there was an armed guard by his side as he said, "Interest rates have gone up and you owe us $4,000 more on last year's payment."

I asked him if he could give me until Monday or Tuesday to get the rest of it to him as it was Friday afternoon at the time.

He said, "Nope. I can't do that. All notes that are due and payable today must be paid in full today," he said, almost mockingly.

My blood was boiling and I knew if I didn't get out of there I was going to crawl across that counter and do something I would regret or, worse yet, I would break down and bawl my eyes out.

To make matters worse, when next Monday rolled around the Federal Land Bank no longer existed and to my knowledge there has never been another bank called "The Federal Land Bank" again.

I gave those thieves my last $20,000 and lost my home and 15 acres of beautiful timber land anyway, as they were pulling out of town.

Talk about throwing salt in an open wound! That stung so bad I can still feel it as I sit and write this account.

I'd never felt so helpless in my life. I had to go home and tell my wife and children that I couldn't keep them in their new home that we had built because of something like "interest" went up and I couldn't pull together another measly 4,000 dollars.

How is a child supposed to understand something like that? How does something like this happen?

What was I supposed to do now? "What is going on in my life?" pounded through my head as I drove the 20 miles home.

Thank God for the Holy Spirit – the Comforter.

As I drove home with this heavy burden on my back I remember sensing Him say, "Trust Me, son. Everything is going to be okay. Just trust me."

From the very beginning of my walk with the Lord I have always repeated aloud everything I sense Him tell me. As I would speak to Him, "Did You say everything is going to be okay? I will trust You Lord; I don't know what else to do right now."

I have always found Him clothing me in His peace.

By the time I got back home I felt His peace and presence with me, which made me feel fine. But then I thought of telling the family and I needed to cry out to Him again.

Every time I did, my cry for help would bring His reassurance – until I finally got to the place where I could go home and tell my family.

"Everything is going to be okay," I stated calmly. "We've just got to trust God for this."

Chapter 3
Cleaning Up My Mess

*S*ome people think that if God is in our lives, all our troubles will go away.

This, however, is *not* the case.

What *is* true is even more exciting than having all our troubles magically disappear.

As sweet as that may seem to be, it would cheat us out of opportunities to know Him by experience, watch Him provide for us and, more importantly, to know ourselves.

God didn't save us to rescue us *from* the trials of life. No, He saved us because we were lost, didn't know who we were and were making messes of our lives in the trials.

He did all He did so He could go through the trials *with* us.

During the late '70s and early '80s American agriculture was going through some incredibly tough times.

Farmers were losing their land because of previously inflated land values, which encouraged bankers to loan farmers some big money in order to expand their operations.

Suddenly the bottom dropped out of land prices as we began going through a horrible recession. Interest rates shot through the roof, crop prices dropped drastically and bankers wanted their loans repaid as originally contracted, and on time.

I was losing everything I had. Plus, I had banked on a fresh crop of lambs and wool to bail us out. But clearly that wasn't working out in any way.

In short, I had a real mess to clean up and I had not a clue what to do. Everything I had ever touched before turned to gold. Now here I was facing something I had never dreamed would ever happen.

My sheep kept dying and nothing on the outside seemed to change. My family was discouraged with a relentless daily diet of doom-and-gloom.

I kept talking to God, trying to persuade Him to do something and I wasn't getting through to Him – or so it seemed.

At that moment I heard nothing. I sensed nothing. And I began to sink once again into absolute despair.

One early morning I was out feeding the sheep and I noticed a ewe and her lamb had died over night.

Suddenly, I lost it. Bigtime.

I threw my pitchfork toward Heaven and uttered some horrible things to God.

"I hate You!" I cried. "You think this is so damn easy, why don't you come down here and try it!"

I was standing on flat ground, screaming as loud as I could, trembling with desperation and rage.

Suddenly my feet went out from under me and I splashed face down into the manure.

Then I heard, "I *did*!"

It sounded like thunder, but there was not a cloud in the sky.

God had answered me with, "I did!"

At that same moment I saw a vision of Jesus hanging on the cross in front of me.

My heart broke and I lay there in the mud and guck weeping and begging Him to forgive me for the bitter, angry venom I was spewing toward Him.

Once again I suddenly felt a calming hand touch my back as He said, "You will be okay, son. Let Me lead you. Follow Me and I will show you the way. Call on Me. Let Me help you. I love you."

I looked up at Him hanging on the cross, blood running down his body, dripping all over me. I sensed Him say, "I did this all for you. I love you son.

"Trust Me!"

How could anyone love another who was using His Name as a swear word, screaming out "I hate You," blaming Him for the economic troubles caused by human greed and yet refusing to go to Him for His compassion, wisdom and help?

Well, it wasn't just anyone on that cross. He was, and is, God. With God all things are possible and I was, and am, outright overjoyed about that fact.

When I was at my weakest point, He came to me and soothed my broken heart.

My sin put the Son of God on that cross that He showed me that day. I knew His invitation was genuine. I also knew He loved me even after all the hatred I was spewing.

For the next two years my days were filled with trying to eke out a living selling commercial light bulbs. During my spare time I worked at cleaning up my farming woes, selling equipment and the remaining livestock while trying to figure out where we were going to live.

The biggest heartache of all was trying to comfort my daughters as their horses were hauled away. I weep as I write this because I know how hard it was on my entire family.

Thank God we stayed together.

Once again the Comforter (Holy Spirit) came to our rescue and those harsh, horrible moments actually turned out to be some of my best memories.

Like lying in the bed of my old pickup truck at midnight with my eight year-old daughter as we ate candy bars and marveled at the beauty of the Milky-Way. (The galaxy, not the candy bar).

It was like we could reach up and touch the stars. We were lost for a few moments in God's universe; far above the pain and struggles of this earthly life.

When things were going relatively well I would forget to call on God. After so long it seemed another problem would surface, and I would blame Him for not holding up His end.

He would then get my attention, soothe me, and invite me to ask Him for guidance. I seemed to be as dense as steel. I just didn't get it that He was able to help me and comfort me through everything.

What a rollercoaster we were on. And I hate roller coasters!

I like strong, steady trips that are well within my control. I hate being up one day and then coming down with a crash, to live depressed, angry and uncertain the next.

I continued down this same trail until the night we went to some friend's house to play Pitch. We usually played for small change just to make the game interesting.

But this night, for some reason, my friend said, "Tonight's losers will take their family to church next Sunday."

"Whoa, that's huge!" I exclaimed. "Are you sure you want to go to church? After all it might cause hell to freeze over when you show up."

We all laughed like fools and started playing cards.

After the second game I could see that this was not going to be my night and I actually began worrying about taking my family to church. After all, we hadn't been to church since our wedding day, and I wasn't sure about this whole thing of church.

I didn't know any of the church goers. What if they ran us out? That would be embarrassing. I just didn't know. I couldn't concentrate on the card game for the worry that was going through my mind.

Suddenly, "Let Me help you!" came into my mind again, and I actually spoke and said, "Oh Lord, help me tonight!"

Everybody thought I was just being funny and they laughed accordingly. But I wasn't kidding. As the games progressed, things got worse and worse for me and my wife.

Dixie never loses in Pitch. She was my ace in the hole, but tonight she wasn't doing any better than I was. Things were not looking good for the Lows for next Sunday. We even began talking about clothes for the girls and I hadn't worn a suit in a very long while.

We were losing!

We talked about the little country church we were going to attend and the pastor who was serving there. We'd heard he spoke in tongues, but didn't teach on it because most of those going to that church didn't believe it was from God.

I thought it strange that people knew he practiced speaking in tongues but didn't believe it was from God – yet they allowed him to have spiritual leadership over their lives!

I openly voiced my opinion with, "What kind of nutcases are going there anyway?"

Our host spoke up, "Oh, we've been there a few times. We like it!"

Ooops! We lost! Plus, I had opened my mouth and inserted my big boorish foot. We didn't win anything the entire night.

I even asked God for help; and what good did it do? Just losers – natural born losers – are what I believed we were as we drove toward home.

We left our friends' home as they laughed, saying, "We'll see you in church tomorrow!"

I couldn't wait to get out of their driveway and scream! I had to go to church in just a few hours.

Ugh!

It had been almost a full year since I had my first experience with Jesus, a big 20-guage shotgun and an instantaneous life change.

L. F. Low

I had never told anybody about my experience, because at that time I didn't know how. It sounded so preposterous. I was afraid no one would believe me and, worse yet, would probably think I was some kind of religious nut or something.

I just kept it to myself. However, I did keep talking to Jesus and allowing the Holy Spirit to pray for me as often as I could; usually during the 45-minute drive to and from Des Moines.

Chapter 4
The Loser Wins

The next day was Sunday and I knew we were not going to church right then. But, for some strange reason, I did feel the draw to eventually go to church.

I didn't understand why at that time.

I reasoned, as I explained to Dixie when we got home, "Tomorrow is Easter and I don't want to be a hypocrite about it like so many people who go on Easter and Christmas and that's it.

"I don't want people to look at us that way, so let's go next week instead."

Well, I didn't say it was a good argument, but it was what was on my mind. So that is the excuse I used to escape one more Sunday.

As I write this I laugh and can't believe I remembered the reason I talked my way out of going on Easter Sunday 1978. But right now it seems like yesterday.

The next Sunday was the big day – the week after Easter, the day hell was going to freeze over.

I had a knot in the pit of my stomach. I felt like I was going to throw up. But here we were, standing outside a little country church.

We were in the middle of nowhere looking up the steps at a big double door that seemed to mock me. Directly above the door a big bell was silent. I felt like they knew we were outside and were trying to be quiet so we would go away.

Dixie grabbed my hand and coaxed, "Come on, you big chicken. Let's go!" And in we went.

As we stepped in from the outside there was another set of double doors we needed to go through and I could hear them talking on the inside. Fear leaped into my throat as Dixie pushed me through the door.

Wow, we did it! And there we stood; my wife Dixie, myself and our three blond daughters ages 15, 12 and 9, all probably looking like five deer in the headlights.

"Whoa," I thought. "We can't leave now; they're all looking right at us!"

The moment the doors swung open, everything stopped. Inside, all 20 people turned to look us over.

The pastor, a kindly old gentleman standing behind the pulpit said, "Please, friends, come in and make yourself at home. You are welcome here."

Everyone seemed to bust themselves to get to us and shake our hand and pat us on the back as if to say, "You made it after all! Welcome."

I don't remember what Pastor Jim preached on that Sunday, but I do remember very clearly what he said to me as we all filed out to go home.

It was the custom for the pastor to shake their hands and bless all the folks who had attended the service as they exited the door.

As Pastor Jim grabbed my hand he looked me square in the eye and said, "I am betting there are a lot of sermons in you, young man! Welcome. It was very good to have you and your beautiful family with us today. Will we see you next week?"

I couldn't believe what I heard myself respond. "You bet," I said. "We will see you next week."

I couldn't believe this had come out of my mouth! I wasn't sorry I had said it, but I was utterly shocked it came so easily.

Actually, I rather looked forward to the next week, as I could sense something huge was cooking and I sensed I was in the middle of it. Even though I didn't fully understand what it was, it was strangely exciting.

I was also very intrigued with his final statement to me, "I'll bet there are a lot of sermons in you!"

"What in the world was that old man saying?" I thought, and kept thinking, for quite some time after that experience.

After attending the church for a couple of months I volunteered to mow the lawn and do some odd jobs around the building. Not too long after that I was also cleaning the building happily.

For some strange reason I felt exhilarated and pleased to be serving the little church in this way. I found myself actually looking forward to cleaning the church building and mowing the yard.

I had this constant feeling that God wanted more for me, but I had no clue what that could be because I didn't know anything about the Bible, and I was still working to get out from under my heavy financial obligations and my failing farm fiasco.

It was in the fall of the same year and the church was busy getting ready for its "Fall Harvest Bazaar" when I asked Pastor Jim if there was anything I could do to help him.

He said, "As a matter of fact there is. I have been meaning to talk to you about something important, so why don't you come by this afternoon and you can help me set up some chairs and then we'll talk."

I had a feeling that he was going to talk to me about serving God in some fashion but I had no notion of what that could be.

I pulled up to the church at the appointed time and went downstairs where Pastor Jim was busy setting up the chairs.

As soon as we finished carrying, cleaning and setting up, we went upstairs and Pastor Jim had a serious look on his face when he said, "Sit down Larry, I need to talk to you."

I felt like I was going to get a lecture on something I was doing wrong.

"It looks like it is serious," I said as I sat down beside him. "What's up?" I asked.

He started right off by saying, "The first day you and your family came to church the Lord spoke clearly to me as all five of you stepped through the door.

"The Lord said to me, 'Here is your Timothy. Disciple him and raise him up for ministry. He will soon take your place.'"

He continued, "Do you remember what I said to you at the door that morning?"

"I sure do," I responded. "You said something about there being many sermons or messages in me."

Pastor Jim smiled warmly. "That's exactly right, Larry. I was referring to what the Lord told me when you walked in. God wants you to pastor his sheep."

You could have pushed me over with a feather at that moment. I stuttered and stammered and finally said, "I could never do that! I don't know anything about the Bible!"

Pastor Jim's response surprised me even more when he said, "That's not my problem. It's the Holy Spirit's problem. He is the Teacher in the Body, not anyone else. Anyway, He told me to disciple you and to prepare you to serve Him."

I had my response ready for him as quickly as a New York defense attorney when I said, "But I like to drink, Pastor Jim. I can afford it and it isn't bothering my family."

Again his response nearly blew me away. He said, "Again, that's not my problem. It's the Holy Spirit's problem. I am only doing what He told me to do.

"Don't worry about all the details right now. God has a plan and you just need to submit to Him and He will do the rest.

"What do you say?"

"What kind of a deal is this?" I thought. "God wants me to serve Him but He doesn't care that I don't know anything and I like to drink? Are you kidding me?"

"Nope, I am not kidding you, Larry. This is what God wants and I am more convinced of it now than I was the day He spoke it to me. God wants you, son. Are you in? Will you let me teach you about ministry? Will you help me?"

I was still pretty young as a Christian but I had learned the standard Christian response, "Can I pray about this before I commit?"

"You sure can," he said. "In fact, I want *you* to hear from the Lord. If you hear from Him and you know it's His idea, you'll be able to go through anything. But if you are not convinced it's from Him, you will cut and run at the first sign of opposition!"

He said this very sternly, but gently. His response, body language and facial expression was telling me that this was exceedingly important and I needed to consider it carefully.

He then prayed for me and asked God to help me line up with His perfect will for my life and then he ended with, "And Lord, if this is not from You, then please forgive me and take the entire thought out of his mind so he doesn't worry. Amen."

Could it really be that God wanted me to shepherd His sheep, but not the four-legged kind? His sheep had only two legs and were more contrary than the wooly type, I was about to learn.

Returning home to get dressed for the evening I kept thinking, "Are you sure, God, that You want me to shepherd Your sheep After all, you know the experience I have recently had with sheep!"

We had a great fall bazaar, ate a lot of food and made lots of money; which, I soon learned, is what a bazaar is supposed to do.

I told Pastor Jim that night that he could count on me to be his Timothy – whoever Timothy was.

I told him I was in! His response? Simple.

"Praise God! Now buckle your seat belt. You are in for an exciting ride."

Chapter 5
Holy Spirit University

*F*rom that day on, for weeks on end, I asked God to send me to bible school. And every time I asked Him, I sensed the same steady answer.

"Just trust Me."

One particular Saturday I had a very strong knowing that I was to join Pastor Jim and allow him to disciple me for ministry.

I was in the basement listening to southern gospel music, trying to recoup from a particularly tough week.

It had become official that the Federal Land Bank was taking our home and I was working with an auctioneer to set up an equipment sale to help me pay off some taxes and some miscellaneous feed bills.

I was feeling terribly defeated and beat-up and I remember thinking how sweet it would be if I could just leave this mess behind, go to bible school and just start all over.

I said, "Lord, I could use a couple of years away, just to get my life started over again. Besides, how am I going to minister to Your sheep if I don't know anything? I haven't got a clue what to do and I am not sure Pastor Jim has enough time to teach me everything I need to learn.

"If you send me to bible school, Lord, I promise I will serve you anywhere you want me to go."

His reply went something like this, "No! I will be your Teacher. You must trust Me!"

His response seemed almost matter-of-fact, yet solemnly final. It ticked me off, and I was about to tell Him to go find someone else because I wasn't going to do it.

Then I sensed Him saying to me, "You must walk through your responsibilities here. I will be with you all the way but you must walk through this the proper way. Your family is depending upon you and you would never be able to live with yourself if you were to walk away now.

"Just trust Me," He said.

I replied, "But Lord, how would You teach me? I need a teacher with some skin on him. I need a diploma or something to show the world that I am educated to minister. How are You going to do that, Lord?" I will never forget His response.

"If you trust Me and follow Me, you will go places and see things the humanly educated can only dream about. Trust Me, son. You can trust Me."

"If I say yes, I don't want to be like everybody else," I said. "Promise me I will be on the cutting edge of what You are doing in the world, Lord. I want to change lives and count for something."

"You can count on Me, son, about anything. Just trust Me."

"When do we start?" I asked Him.

"Join me at four a.m. Monday morning," He said.

Four in the morning? Are you kidding me? I didn't know there was life before six!

So I said, "You've got to wake me up, Lord. I am not going to set my alarm and disturb my family."

‧I felt a sense of exhilaration and hope from my communication with the Lord; which was a far cry from what I was feeling before we began to talk.

I ran upstairs to tell my wife about this time I had just had with the Lord and her response was, "That's fine for you, but just don't wake me up at four a.m."

I assured her gently that *if* it took place, I would not disturb her.

* * *

I honestly never gave it another thought the remainder of the weekend. I even went to bed Sunday night without a thought of getting up early; I set my alarm at the usual six a.m. and went to bed.

Suddenly, in the middle of the night, my eyes popped open and I was wide awake. I looked at the alarm clock and you probably already know what time it was. Yep – four a.m. straight up.

I got suddenly excited as I got out of bed, went to the bathroom, brushed my teeth and combed my hair.

People have asked me, "Why did you do that?"

My response: "I wanted to look presentable to the Lord *if* He showed up."

From that day on I even took my shower and got dressed; after all, I was going to bible school.

Downstairs, I went to my office; a little room sitting in the middle of the basement with no outside windows. It was to double as a safe haven during storms, so it was built to withstand the effects of a nothing less than a tornado.

I opened the door and went inside, sat at my desk and said, "Here I am, Lord."

I instantly sensed His presence. The Head Master was in the classroom. He instantly began teaching me as Scriptures began coming to me.

As each Scripture came to mind I looked it up and read it. I then wrote a paragraph or two as to what the scripture was teaching me. Some of my paragraphs were only a line or two, as this was all brand new to me.

I literally felt like a giddy freshman student in his first day of college; fearful of missing something, attentive and excited.

I followed this exercise, looking up the Scriptures, reading them and writing something about them for my first hour, my heart beating rapidly. I recognized the Teacher was right there in my basement office and I was His most ardent pupil.

Suddenly I realized I had never turned on the lights. But it didn't matter. My room was lit up with the softest, clearest light I had ever witnessed.

I had no idea what it was or why my room was aglow until sometime later when I learned about the Shekinah glory of God and how Moses actually lit up when he was in the presence of the Lord.

I also read later about the transfiguration of Jesus when He glowed brightly with God's Shekinah glory on the mountain top, meeting with Moses and Elijah.

I was sitting there basking in God's great Shekinah glory – His presence!

I don't know why I did what I did next. I got up and turned on the light. I then turned it off and my room was dark as you would expect it to be.

I have often wondered since that moment if the Lord would have continued to light up my room each day as we met there?

If only I had not flipped that switch!

Was He just trying to show me that He can be trusted and He was actually there?

I think so, because I continued to meet Him in that room every Monday through Friday from 4 to 6 a.m. for the next two years.

Why only on weekdays? It's because He never woke me early on Saturdays or Sundays.

I remember specific lessons through the books of 1st and 2nd Timothy. I learned who Timothy was and how he related to the Apostle Paul. Suddenly I saw it; Pastor Jim had said, "You are my Timothy."

Then it became clear to me. I got it that Pastor Jim was my Paul and I was set to be his Timothy.

I never claimed to be the sharpest knife in the drawer, but I did – finally – get it!

We spent a great deal of time in the Gospels, especially in the Gospel of John and the books of 1st, 2nd and 3rd John.

In the two years we went through every book in the Bible, but some of the lessons stand out more to me today than others.

It was a wonderful, exciting time as the Holy Spirit taught me how to minister, how to trust Him, how to surrender, how to communicate with Him, how to walk in faith and just believe.

Looking back over my time in the classroom with Him, I realize He has shown me how much of what I learned wasn't really learned at all.

It was downloaded.

Much of the time I found myself sitting in His awesome presence, literally feeling the weight of His benevolence on me.

During those times I would be afraid to move for fear it would disturb the moment. Many times my flesh would cry out by telling me I was thirsty. Other times my mind would remind me of a million things I needed to be doing.

If at any time I would give in to the urging of my flesh (get a drink, make a note about something I needed to do or get something to eat) the moment would be broken and I would always feel incomplete.

I now know it was during these times that the Lord was downloading information He knew I would need in both the near and distant future.

I began recognizing I was very confident. I knew things that I couldn't remember the source of, or the time of learning it. As I would be preaching or teaching a bible study, information that fit and was needed would come out of my mouth with confidence and clarity that would astound me.

After class I would ask the Lord where I got that information and He would show me the times I sat quietly in His presence and He would say, "I downloaded it to you, son."

Look for a minute at Jeremiah 33:3,

"Call to Me, and I will answer you, and show you great and mighty things which you do not know."

The Message translation says it this way.

"Call to Me and I will answer you. I'll tell you marvelous and wondrous things that you could never figure out on your own."

The original words are, "I will give you unsearchable truths you have no other way of finding out."

The Lord likened it to the Hebrews in the desert escaping from Egypt when He told them to pick up just enough manna for the day. They couldn't pick up more than they would need for that day or it would spoil and be no good when they needed it.

He had told me, "As you spend time with me, each day I am able to download what only I know you will need."

There would be days when I would instinctively know what He was giving me so I could write it down. Much revelation came that way.

However, there were many times when I would not know anything was being downloaded. During those times I was obviously in His presence, but there were no words being exchanged between us.

As I left those sessions, I would always feel invigorated. But I wouldn't have a clue what else I had received. I did learn that when I had those moments, He was downloading. And when I was released I just thanked Him for the time He gave me.

We can have those moments as often as we like. He is always willing to spend time with us. Sometimes it takes time, but the Lord told me, "Time spent with Me is never a waste of time. I will always return you hours of productivity for the minutes you give Me."

I have gotten into a habit of starting my day with thinking of a particular time when I met Him and knew He helped me. The time I think of varies from day to day.

As I recall the day I always thank Him for what He has done for me. I praise Him and love Him with words of appreciation, praise and adoration.

During these times I suddenly feel the tingling of His presence begin to settle on me. As His presence intensifies, I begin to sit very still; I know He is doing something in me, whether I understand at that moment or not. I know I will know later when it counts.

Looking back over the fits I once threw because the Lord would not allow me to go to bible school embarrasses me. I am so richly blessed to say that what I now teach was not taught to me by any man.

The Holy Spirit has been and always will be my teacher. He has promised to lead us and guide us into all truth and He does not speak of Himself or on His own.

He tells us everything that the Lord Jesus gives Him to say. Therefore, I have been taught by Jesus Himself.

Thank you, Lord!

This has been my time in HSU – Holy Spirit University. I have never graduated from HSU, nor do I expect I will until He takes me out of this world and I stand face to face with Him in all His glory.

However, I have received my PHD because I know that I am currently Past Having Doubts when it comes to trusting Him with the details of my life and ministry.

My education continues daily, all day. I just don't meet Him at four a.m. anymore.

* * *

Finally, the Federal Land Bank couldn't seem to do without our home, even though they hadn't been in business for a couple of years at this point.

We had to move out, so we moved to town and rented a house, called the "big house," on the corner.

We lived there for a few years and then the Lord made a way for us to acquire our own home that we still own to this day.

Moving was very sad and my daughters were very angry with the people who had the dirty job of keeping us moving. I had my hands full with the actual move and trying to keep my family and myself from acquiring a bitter heart.

It was very hard on all of us, but we did it. We held our heads high and walked through it, all with the Lord's help.

Without Him it could have gotten ugly.

People often say, "What doesn't kill you makes you stronger." I believe that now, for certain.

While living in that big house on the corner we were serving as pastor to our first church and we had our share of trials. One of our biggest trials was the loss of our first grandchild who passed away before his third day of life.

While living in this house I went to Mexico to minister for a couple of weeks, saw many miracles and almost died. During those few years I am proud to say that my life was threatened for preaching the Gospel.

And when the big house on the corner sold we had no place to go for a while. But we watched the Lord open the doors required to give us a new home.

I mention all these things not to inspire pity, because they were nothing that people don't experience every day somewhere and everywhere in the world.

I mention them to let the world know that these misfortunes *did* make us stronger and more capable of ministering and appreciating each other and the presence of the Lord in our lives.

Without these experiences we wouldn't be the people we are today.

I want people to know that Holy Spirit will take care of them should they be in a similar situation.

God is good!

Chapter 6
The Name Above All Names

"The Spirit of the Lord God is upon Me... to proclaim liberty to the captives and opening of the prison to those who are bound;" (Isaiah 61:1b, c)

*I*t was a night not fit for man or beast that steamy Iowa summer's evening in July of 1984.

We were being hammered by a whopping storm – tremendous thunder claps, along with explosive lightning flashes, fortified by wicked wind and torrential rain – when I received a call from a neighbor.

He proceeded to ask if I would be willing to go, immediately, to the hospital to help his ailing mother, whose name was Amilda.

At that time I didn't personally know the woman, as both of this man's parents attended another church in a neighboring town. So naturally I inwardly questioned his confidence in my ability to assist much in such a personal family matter.

I sensed, though, a genuine urgency and no small fear in his voice. I asked him to tell me about his mother's behavior and emotional state. He reported that earlier that very night she had been committed by other family members to a mental hospital.

"She's not crazy," he insisted. "But she won't speak. She's in there all alone and she won't talk to anyone, not even her pastor. But she is not insane, she's just completely *silent*. Would you *please* go see if you can help her?"

He told me a bit about his family, and I surmised that while there were serious problems between his parents, they didn't seem to be so horrendous as to warrant having her committed – at least at first glance.

I told him I'd call the hospital to see if such a late visit was allowed. It was already past 9 p.m. and I secretly hoped they would tell me I couldn't come until the next day.

It was storming like a Hollywood sound stage and I had never been to a mental hospital before, willingly or otherwise. I had no idea what to expect.

I let my imagination get a little carried away, I'm afraid, as their phone rang. I saw myself waiting in the raging night at a towering steel-reinforced door that separated the "sane" from the raving *in*sane.

Lightning strikes seared the sky; wolves howled maniacally and too close for comfort as the rain pounded down in vast, slashing sheets.

I could almost hear the door creek opening ever so slowly to reveal two beady yellow eyes peering through the crack in the dark and eerily querying, in true Draculian style,

"Good *ee*ven-ing. How may I serve you?"

As the plot of my horror film thickened in my head, I nevertheless was able to realize I was calling a mental hospital, not a modern day chamber of horrors.

"Wow," I mused. "It's amazing the strange and wonderful things the mind can conjure in one's zeal to serve God!"

I introduced myself to the attending nurse as a pastor of the family, and by her smooth and steady voice I could tell she was smiling.

"You are more than welcome to come tonight," she assured brightly. "Enter through the emergency entrance; take the elevator to the fourth floor. We'll be waiting for you."

So much for Dracula's castle!

I got dressed, kissed my wife good bye, grabbed an umbrella and headed to my car between lightning bolts. Then I sped toward the hospital.

The rain pelted down so intensely the windshield wipers didn't stand a chance. Lightening glared at times so brightly my eyes wouldn't focus. Wind gusts blasted as it streaked across the sky in front of and all around me; which pushed my already humming imagination into overdrive.

As I pulled up to the hospital, I was surprised to find a well-lit parking lot outside a modern hospital, not a steel-barred gate separating me from a decrepit and intimidating old fortress.

I even found a parking place right next to the emergency entrance that was marked Pastors Only.

Things were looking up.

As I entered, I met the night guard who directed me to the elevator with a welcoming smile and a, "Have a good evening, Pastor." I began to feel almost comfortable about this. The guard didn't have a limp, a grotesque scar on his forehead or a Transylvanian accent. He was just a regular fella like me.

I reminded myself that I was nevertheless in a facility for the mentally ill and had better keep on my toes. Didn't the Bible say to be alert and pray on all occasions? So I continued praying, more out of apprehension and uncertainty than in preparation to minister.

When I got to the fourth floor and the elevator doors opened, I saw a glistening stainless steel door across from a waiting area. Two nurses stood by the door. As I approached, one of them said, "Good evening, Pastor Larry. We're glad you made it! Was it a horrible drive?"

I was shocked they knew my name! My mind started to race again. I became convinced I was about to encounter my worst nightmare.

They knew my name and I hadn't even opened my mouth – they had read my mind! That's just spooky! I had forgotten, of course, that I gave my name and the reason for my visit to the night guard.

He had called ahead to the ward by telephone, not by sending a grunting Igor up a secret passage or tying a note to the feet of a rabid bat or a mad carrier raven.

The nurse on duty ushered me inside, explaining that they hadn't been able to extract *any* reactions out of Amilda since she'd been admitted – not a single word, sound, expression or gesture to indicate why or how she arrived at her condition.

She was just blank, they said, staring into space, oblivious to her surroundings.

To my relief, the room was video-monitored. If I should need anything, all I had to do was holler. I would be on camera, and the staff would keep a watchful eye on the proceedings.

They had tried every psychological trick in the book to get Amilda to indicate, in *whatever* way, what might be the matter.

As the head nurse opened the door to Amilda's room, a chill shot down my back. She appeared all but catatonic – barely alive, said the nurse.

I began to wonder what I could do here. If the doctors, nurses and all the highly trained counselors couldn't get a peep out of her, what could I do? Naturally I started to beat up on myself.

"You dummy," I muttered. "When are you are going to learn to say 'No'?"

I looked around the room and saw and heard nothing and no one. The room was empty as far as I could tell, but I knew I wasn't alone. I saw that the bed was quite a distance from the wall, so I mustered enough courage to look on the floor between them.

There I found her, cowering in the corner, rolled up in a tight ball, not saying a word or moving even a finger. She barely even blinked!

"Amilda, can you hear me?" I asked. No response. "Amilda, may we talk?" No response. She didn't budge. Then I stood up and implored, aloud, "Lord, what do I do?"

Instantly I sensed the Holy Spirit say, "And every knee must bow and every tongue must confess, that Jesus Christ is Lord to the glory of the Father." The emphasis was on *every* knee and *every* tongue responding to the Name of Jesus.

With that Word of Knowledge new hope surfaced from deep in my heart and I eagerly looked over across the bed again and asked, "Amilda, do you know Jesus?"

Just as I got those five short words out of my mouth, she looked up and said, clearly and emphatically, "Well, yes. I do!"

"Well then, come on up here and let's talk about Him!" I cried. As soon as I invited her up to talk about Jesus, she sprang from behind that bed like a person half her age.

She sat on the edge of her bed and I sat in a facing chair. We began to talk about Jesus. She didn't know who I was, and I had never seen her before. But we had instant fellowship and the fears that had forced her in there began to melt away.

She told me that something came over her about a month prior. She was certain that everyone wanted to kill her. She said she remembered the moment it happened – it was like a "thick, dark blanket" had dropped down and she was deathly afraid for her life.

I asked her why she didn't ask to talk to her pastor and she said that she couldn't remember his name – or anyone else's, for that matter. Yet she had this desperate, overpowering feeling that everyone, family and close friends alike, wished her dead.

I asked her why she wasn't afraid of me and she said, "Because you know Jesus! The moment you said 'Do you know Jesus?' all my fears just lifted. I'm not afraid anymore!"

We prayed together and bound up her spirits of fear and paranoia while we loosed them from duty against her (Matthew 18:18). We then asked God for her complete healing according to 1Peter 2:24 and that the doctors recognize the miracle of her recovery.

My mission, just like that, was complete.

As the nurse accompanied me out the main door, she said, "I've never seen *anything* like that before. No one has been able to get the slightest reaction out of her since she came in here. Now *you* get her to respond in the first five minutes!"

I told her it wasn't me. It was the Name of Jesus and the power of God that freed her from her fears.

"Amilda is completely healed now," I told her. She looked at me with suspicion.

"Well, we'll let the doctors determine that!" she laughed. "Good night." Then she shut the door behind me.

I knew she didn't understand what I had just told her. I wasn't totally sure I did either.

As I headed home, the Lord showed me the wonderful and awesome power of the Name of Jesus. It suddenly became a reality to me that in those few quick seconds, just the *mention* of the Name of Jesus had completely released Amilda from her personal prison of incapacitating, inexplicable fear.

I was sure that no one, until that moment, had even thought to mention the Name of

Jesus to her. If they had, they could've seen the same miracle I had just been a part of.

The day after my visit to Amilda was Sunday. After church I went back to the hospital to see her. When I got to the fourth floor, the elevator doors opened and there was Amilda and her entire family. This time, they were all *outside* the steel door.

As I got off the elevator, her husband and son came running to shake my hand and emotionally thank me for visiting her in the storm of the previous night.

"Pastor, Mama's okay!" her son rejoiced. "The doctors can find no reason to keep her! She's back to her old self. She's come back to us. She's okay!"

She sure was! I talked to Amilda and she was nothing less than focused, bright-eyed and raring to get back into her life, and smiling splendidly.

We prayed with the whole family and thanked God for the miracle-working power in the Name of our Lord Jesus Christ.

"Therefore God also has highly exalted Him and given Him the Name which is above every name, which is the Name of Jesus. Every knee should bow, of those in Heaven, and of those on earth. And of those under the earth and that every tongue should confess that Jesus Christ is Lord, to the glory of God the Father."
(Philippians 2:9-11)

Amilda came back to real life basically because I had no idea of what to do so I just asked God for His help and followed His instructions.

"If any of you lacks wisdom, let him ask of God, Who gives to all liberally and without reproach, and it will be given to Him." (James 1:5)

"Jesus healed me!" Amilda yodeled to them on her way out. And the nurse on duty that night will never be able to say, "I didn't know!"

The Bible is very clear; all it takes is a regular guy willing to submit to God's plan.

* * *

I worked with Pastor Jim Patrick for four years while working in Des Moines making a living, attending Holy Spirit University.

On the 26th day of November, 1984 the Board of Trustees and the church body of this little country community church voted and unanimously agreed that I should be their next Lead Pastor.

During those four years we established a youth ministry, I experienced a couple of weddings and ministered two funerals, an ice cream social and two fall bazaars on my own, plus the miracle with Amilda.

Holy Spirit said I was ready!

During the next four years serving this church I also wrapped up my secular profession as the Holy Spirit opened doors to many people's hearts where I was blessed to lead over 200 individuals to the saving knowledge of Jesus Christ.

People were always seeking me out to share their stories with me. During those meetings, usually during lunch or after work, the Holy Spirit would have them convinced they should also know Jesus personally and I was more than willing to be His vessel.

The Holy Spirit constantly glorifies Jesus while He is convicting the sinners of their need for Him.

He is amazing!

Chapter 7
For As We Think We Are

"For as he thinks in his heart, so is he."
(Proverbs 23:7a)

Our minds are tremendously powerful.

In fact, what you believe about yourself is what you have become – and what you shall become.

What is so good about this statement is that if you don't like what you have become, you can change it by changing what you believe about yourself.

This is exactly what happened to a woman who shuffled into my office one day. This is Linda's story.

During my last secular position I was responsible for hiring a staff of computer specialists for a special project. It wasn't long after I took the position that the human resources department called to tell me that an applicant for one of the positions was there waiting for her interview.

Her hair was hanging down over her face as she looked straight down at her feet. She shuffled like a lobotomized mental patient.

Immediately my mind said, "No way, Jose." But out of courtesy I felt I owed her an opportunity to tell her story. After all, she got through HR and I didn't think they would send her up for a joke.

I greeted her and she stuck out her hand without looking up at me. As I shook her hand I cordially asked her to have a seat.

She sat down, never once looking at me, and I had to ask her for the file in her hand. As I took the file from her hand and began to read her resume my mind was a blur.

It was illegible. I could not make hide nor hair of it.

I genuinely suspected that someone sent her to me as a joke to see how I would respond. It was well known that I was a Christian pastor at the time, and there were several in this business that didn't look kindly on my faith and the fact that I was in charge.

"What are you here for? Who sent you?" I asked, fully expecting for her to raise her head and begin laughing at my confusion.

She responded very quietly as she looked at me for the first time, "Human Resources sent me up. I'm sorry to waste your time, Mr. Low. I thought maybe I could get a job here."

Her response, demeanor, and sincerity broke my heart. So I invited her to tell me about her background before I sent her away.

As Linda began telling me about her tech skills I just couldn't focus on what she said because of what she looked like.

I couldn't help myself and I blurted out, "Why do you dress this way? Why do you walk the way you do? You dress and walk like an old lady! You are not an old lady. Why do you do this?"

Then I apologized for my abrupt questions, but she surprisingly said, "Don't worry about it. Everybody looks at me funny and I really didn't want to come today because I knew how I would be received. But my parents said I needed to get a job and begin taking care of myself."

I looked at the fact sheet and it said she was 45 years old. She was older than I was and she was still living at home. "Unbelievable!" I thought as I asked her, "So you still live with your parents?"

"Yes I do, ever since I got out of the hospital the last time."

"I am sorry you have been sick. How long were you in the hospital?" I asked.

Her response almost bowled me over; "Off and on for over 34 years."

I thought, "That's it. I can reject her because of her health. You've got to be healthy to work here. I am sure she will understand my reasoning."

"Why so long?" I asked.

"I've been under psychiatric care since I was 13 years old. I have to visit my psychiatrist every week and once a month I go to the hospital for tests."

I felt like I had just been let off the hook and was about to explain to her why she wouldn't fit in with our team when I sensed the Lord say, "I want you to hire this poor, unfortunate woman."

I am sure I had a funny look on my face as I recognized it was God who sent her to me. I told her I would need to pray about my decision and would have HR call her tomorrow with my decision.

All that evening the Lord kept telling me to hire her. I asked Him why, but never received an answer until I was on my way to work the next morning.

As I pulled into the parking lot the Lord impressed upon me one last time to hire her and when I asked why He said, "Because you need her."

I had no idea what that meant, but I knew He was very emphatic about it and I did not wish to disobey the Lord. Without thinking about it any further, I went straight to my phone and called HR informing them of my decision, expecting them to laugh at me.

The HR director said, "Thank you, Mr. Low. We will inform her. Do you wish her to report right away? She has no commitments at this time."

"Yes," I replied. "Let's start her next Monday." Then I hung up the phone wondering what in the world was going on.

Monday morning came more quickly that week than any other week and the first one in my office was Linda.

I explained to her that she would be a part of a team and to be accepted by the team she would need to, well, fix herself up a bit; hair, business clothes, shoes – pretty much a complete make-over.

She began to cry and explained she didn't know how to go shopping for any of that.

I wanted to say a lot, but nothing seemed appropriate at that moment. So I called another young lady who was a Christian and had been working with me for a while and asked her to help Linda go shopping.

She was happy to help, praise the Lord.

As time went on I noticed two things about Linda – one good and one not so good. First of all she was brilliant as a computer programmer and secondly she was extremely negative about practically everything, especially about herself.

After she worked with us for a couple of weeks she was beginning to feel a little more comfortable and she had a solid new friend in the young lady who helped her shop.

For the sake of the team and the job we had to do, I had a little talk with her about her negativity. When I approached her about the subject she seemed surprised that I thought she was negative.

I asked her young friend to join us as I wanted to speak to her about her demeanor. I asked her if she was okay physically, especially concerning how she walked.

She said she was fine, so I asked her friend to help her learn to walk with her head held high and not to shuffle but to walk heal-toe, heal-toe.

We both shared areas in which she was down on herself. She constantly called herself a psycho and a schizo. She was always down on herself when corrected for anything.

Her response was, "I only believe what I have been told my whole life."

She had been diagnosed with paranoid schizophrenia, bi-polar depression, social anxiety disorder, and the list continued. She had been taking anti-psychotic medications since that time to the tune of 30 plus pills a day.

A few were the anti-psychotic meds and the remaining pills were to offset what the psych meds were doing to her liver, kidneys and stomach.

She was told that she would never be any better, but the doctors said they would help her *cope* with her condition.

She said, with tears in her eyes, "I call myself those things because that's what I've been told I am. And I can't help what I am."

I asked her if that is what she wanted to remain and she said, "Not at all! That's why I continue to see my psychiatrist every week. I want to change but nothing works for me! "

"Are you willing to try something you obviously haven't tried?" I asked.

"Yes. Anything! I'll try anything!" she said as emphatic as I'd seen her.

I told her I thought she was a brilliant computer programmer and had a great future, but she was doing herself great harm believing negatively about herself.

I asked her to find those derogatory labels in the Bible and she said, visibly embarrassed, "You know they're not in there."

I told her that if she really wanted to change – that is, be healed – from this moment on I didn't want to hear her refer to herself with any label that wasn't in the Bible.

From that day on I had her memorize Scriptures that said she was holy, forgiven, accepted in the beloved, chosen, loved, redeemed, valuable, without blame and living in the righteousness of God.

Occasionally she would feel sick and get down on herself. While praying for her one day, the Lord helped me see that as her beliefs changed her body was also changing (Proverbs 14:30) and her medications were causing her to feel ill and overdosed.

I suggested that to her and she went to the doctor where they did a blood work-up and found she was being over-medicated. With each trip to the doctor they would reduce the amount of meds she was on.

It seemed that Linda changed physically every day after she began believing what God had to say about her. There was such a change in her countenance that others in our building began asking what was up.

Linda walked like everybody else, her head held high. She began glowing with self-awareness. It was amazing to see this human metamorphosis taking place in front of us.

After several years of this, one day she returned from the doctor, absolutely aglow. It was almost like she floated into the office.

With tears in her eyes and her voice shaking, she told us that the psychiatrist she had been seeing every week since she was 13 told her she didn't need to come see him anymore.

She reported the doctor saying, "I don't know what you have been doing these past few years, but whatever it is, please keep it up – because as far as I can see, you are a rare phenomenon!

"You have healed, you're off all medications and there is nothing more I can do for you. In all of my years of practice I have never seen anything like this. You are more sane than *I* am right now."

I asked her what she told him and she said, "I told him that all I have done is memorize Scripture and begin to believe what God has to say about me."

As a person believes in their heart, so they are. We had a party for Linda to help her celebrate being freed from over 35 years of bondage.

What is a rare phenomenon to the world should be common, everyday occurrences to believers. The Holy Spirit's job is to lead us and guide us into all truth and righteousness with the ultimate goal of perfect inner peace and freedom.

Chapter 8
What You Ask In My Name

"Most assuredly, I say to you, he who believes in Me, the works that I do he will do also; and greater works than these he will do, because I go to My Father." (John 14:12)

*I*t was October 1985 when I met Kelly's mom in the break room at my office. I had recently become acquainted with her during a meeting we both attended just the day before.

She was standing at the coffee vending machine, crying. I asked her if she was all right, or if I could help her in any way.

My question and offer to help triggered a floodgate of tears and opened the door to one of the greatest miracles I have ever been blessed to be a part of.

Her name was Ellen, and as she began to openly weep, she explained that she had a 21 year-old daughter who was dying.

Kelly was her name, and Ellen explained that she had been suffering from anorexia and bulimia since she was 13, which drove her into the drug scene, and she was now a full-fledged cocaine addict.

Suddenly, out of my mouth I heard the words, "Ellen, God does not want your daughter to die and I think He will heal her."

She looked at me with a startled look and said, "I hope you're right."

Before I could even think, I said, "If I can be of any help, don't be afraid to let me know. I don't know for sure what I could do, but I would be willing to go see her, because God does not want her to die."

At that, Ellen went to the women's room to freshen up and I found myself heading down the long hall to my office.

"Boy, you did it this time. What are you going to do if they call you to go see their daughter?" kept running through my mind. "What can you do? Boy you've stepped in it now!" ...and on and on.

I knew these thoughts were not from God because they were so condemning. But it was just that I couldn't believe I would be so bold about such a serious situation with a woman I hardly knew.

It would have been different if Ellen went to my church. At least then I would have some sort of idea what she knew about God. I didn't even know if she believed in divine healing or anything else!

No, I had to pick on a complete stranger and, worse yet, someone who worked in the same office building as I did. I could just see it now; Ellen would tell everybody what I had said, her daughter would die and I would be left looking like a religious jerk with a mouth bigger than my faith.

I was overcome by fear – all because of the compassion I felt for the poor mother who was about to lose her young daughter. She had evidently suffered many years with a broken heart because of their relationship and her daughter's issues.

Because of that fear I began to pray in my spirit language. Quietly and under my breath I frantically prayed in the Spirit so I could regain some peace and begin to hear God over the jeering of my flesh which, at that moment, had turned me into a king-sized coward.

The rest of the week went by and I didn't see Ellen at all. The following Thursday morning, I was in my office early when I heard someone come into the outer office and ask the secretaries, "Is Larry in yet?"

I recognized that voice even though I had only heard it a couple of times. My heart began to beat double-time. Without even slowing down, Ellen came straight for my office like a woman on a mission.

I can remember my heart and stomach coming up into my throat at once, and the condemning thoughts ran rampant.

"This is it, Preacher Boy," they warned. "She is going to have you for lunch. Her daughter died and she is coming to find out why! What are you going to tell her? You are going to look like a fool!"

I just started pleading with God for the words to say to this bereaved and possibly angry mother and there she was, standing in my doorway.

I could tell Ellen had been crying and I knew she wasn't there to give me good news.

She dove right in without any hesitation.

"Last night my husband and I went to talk to Kelly's doctor, and he said Kelly was dying for sure, and that she would be dead by the weekend. He told us to notify the family before then."

She went on to explain why Kelly was dying. She said, "Kelly is no longer able to take food orally and her veins have collapsed. So they can no longer feed her through an I.V. Her stomach is destroyed, so they can't feed her with a stomach tube. Kelly has given up all hope and she doesn't want to live any longer."

The next question sent a chill down my spine, even though I had expected it from the beginning.

"Would you go see her?" she cried. "They have pushed her into a corner to die!"

Without even thinking (thank God the Holy Spirit can speak through us at times without allowing us to think – or we would talk ourselves out of serving God in times like these) I said, "You know I will."

In the next few seconds, Ellen gave me the particulars on how to find Kelly and said that she would call hospital security on the eating disorder ward and give them my name so I could get in to see her.

The moment Ellen left my office I began to make calls. "*Help!* I need you to pray!" I cried to everyone who would listen.

During the entire day, I paced back and forth in my office, praying in my spirit language when I would get a call or have to go check on something. I would pray in the Spirit as I walked to my meetings. I took lunch by myself and found a quiet place in the building to sit quietly with God and pray in the Spirit.

At times like this, we do not know how to pray. We always desire to see miracles, but how does one pray to make sure one sees it!

Only God knows. And no one knows the things of God except the Spirit of God (1 Corinthians 2:11).

Remember, we cannot muster up, or force, the power of God. We can only prepare ourselves to *receive* it. How do we do that? We pray in the Holy Spirit. By humbling ourselves, admitting we do not know how to pray as we ought to (Romans 8:26), we empty ourselves and allow the Spirit of God to refill us with His power by praying in the Holy Spirit.

This is exactly what happens when we pray in tongues and is what the Apostle Paul was teaching us in 1 Corinthians 14:2-4 and Jude 20 when he said that when you pray in tongues you "edify yourself" or "build yourself up."

By the time I got off work, I was ready and very excited about going to visit this young lady. I had spent the entire day praying more than working, asking God to help me be a blessing. I asked God to give me courage and the wisdom to know what to do.

God, in turn, gave me His peace that passes all understanding. I was ready to go!

When I got to the hospital, I went directly to the proper floor and had no trouble finding the door that separated the patients in the eating disorder ward from the rest of the patients and visitors.

I rang the bell and in a few seconds a nurse asked for my name and who I was there to visit. I told her, and then silence.

A few seconds later the door opened and the nurse said, "Pastor Low, please follow me." She then turned and immediately led me down the hall to Kelly's room.

What I am about to describe I found out over several weeks following this initial visit. I had no way of knowing all this during the first visit and Ellen hadn't expounded on how serious her daughter was.

As I entered her room I was met with the stench of death and rotting flesh. Kelly was in bed and I would have bet anything she was dead. At least that's what she looked and smelled like.

Kelly had not had any nourishment – that she would allow to stay in her system – for over 40 days. As people would make her eat, she would immediately find a way to purge it out of her digestive system before it could do her any good.

As she ended this particular 40 days, Kelly stole several boxes of laxatives from a local drug store and began to eat them, in a desperate attempt to make sure she would not gain any weight.

She successfully consumed 45 laxatives which sent her body into toxic shock, resulting in a coma and causing her stomach to begin digesting itself in an attempt to supply food for her starved body.

I was about to get a crash course on this terrible sickness that plagues our modern society – about the pain and suffering that beautiful, young women and handsome young men put themselves through in an attempt to meet the expectations of the Barbie and Ken image that society seems to favor.

Kelly just wanted to look pretty, with no fat or excess of any kind on her body. Her mind told her that she was fat and ugly, so Kelly did everything in her power to get the excess weight off.

When our minds become filled with lies perpetrated by life's experiences – and misinterpretations of them – we are filled with pain.

Lies – like, we are ugly, or stupid or too fat – are so powerful and so effective that, in her case, Kelly went from a normal 5' 3" teenager that was a little overweight, down to a 64-pound cocaine addict trying to control her pain, and very obviously dying.

Her blood pressure could no longer be detected through the conventional arm cuff method. Her internal body temperature was 85 degrees, her eyes were recessed deep into her skull and the pupils were cloudy and white.

Her hair was wispy, thin and very short. It was easy to see that her hair had also suffered from the lack of nourishment. Her abdominal area was swollen so large that I thought she must be pregnant and in her final trimester.

I found out days later that her stomach had been completely eaten up by digestive juices. Her bowel was also damaged along with her bladder, womb and ovaries. She hadn't had a bowel movement or been able to urinate for several weeks and she was unable to receive any kind of nourishment.

Kelly was just hours from death and very silent!

She was in pain, afraid of death and angry. She definitely did not want to see a preacher.

I truly thought she was dead until I spoke to her. She came alive, spewing all kinds of words that came from a hurting, broken heart that definitely convinced me that she did not want to talk to me, or anyone else.

As I stood there in shock, listening to all this filth, trying desperately to keep from vomiting from the smell in that room, Holy Spirit said, "Shut her mouth in Jesus' Name."

I repeated that command and as I did, Kelly's mouth clamped shut with a pop and she looked straight at me through those cloudy, vacant eyes.

I began to minister to her as Holy Spirit led and after what seemed like only a couple of minutes, tears began to flow without her making a sound.

I then began praying with her to receive Jesus as her personal Savior.

I was holding her hands as we prayed at the end of that quick prayer, and without looking up, Kelly said, "Do you think God would heal me?"

At that same moment the Lord spoke to my heart and said, "I just did. Just praise Me!"

I told Kelly, "The Lord just did heal you! Let's thank Him and praise Him."

I was still holding her hands and suddenly I felt her ice-cold, bony hands begin to grow warm. Kelly said, "I have never felt this good in my life. I tingle all over!"

As she spoke that to me, I looked at her eyes and suddenly the cloudy mist covering them left like two wisps of smoke being blown away by a gentle breeze. Her eyes began to sparkle and shine and were deep, dark brown. I remember I was shocked to see my reflection in them just before she began to gently cry.

God had healed Kelly and she knew it! She came out of that bed laughing and crying, overjoyed with what was taking place in her body. We prayed and thanked God. We laughed and cried together and then we praised God some more for what was happening in that room at that very moment.

We still didn't know the full extent of what God was doing, and wouldn't know until the following morning.

I left the hospital and hurried home to prepare for a Bible study I was teaching that night. I was running late, so I had very little time to share what I had just witnessed with my wife.

Later on that night, after the bible study, I tried to explain it all to her, but it seemed so preposterous to me by that time that I wondered myself if I had been dreaming.

No wonder she merely smiled and said, "At least she's going to Heaven now. Praise God for that."

In the middle of the night I was awakened suddenly. As I opened my eyes there was light in our room like as if a television was on. We had no television in our room. I sat up in bed and suddenly I saw on the wall a life-size vision of Jesus healing Kelly.

God turned the entire wall of our bedroom into a giant television screen so I could see what was happening in the hospital.

I saw Jesus and He seemed to fill Kelly's room. His hands and part of His forearms were submerged into Kelly's lower back. Kelly was in bed, lying on her stomach with her hands folded together under her right cheek as she slept.

She was wearing a black and gold University of Iowa football jersey as a night shirt and it had the number 69 on the back. There was no movement in this vision, but I knew in a flash what was going on.

When God gives you an open-eyed vision like that there is no confusion. You know what He is doing and what you are supposed to do with it.

The next morning I couldn't wait to get to the hospital to see what had happened.

Although I felt I knew, I had to see it with my own eyes.

When I got to Kelly's room, there she was, standing in front of her mirror, combing her beautiful, auburn, shoulder-length hair.

I remembered that the night before, her hair was wispy, short, and very thin and I thought it was sort of mousy gray. It certainly wasn't shiny, auburn and hanging past her shoulders. It was beautiful! She was beautiful. A bright glow surrounded her.

"What happened to you?" I asked her.

With tears in her eyes she said, "Jesus healed me."

I said, "I know. I saw Him do it." I told her what I had seen in my vision that night and when I got to the description of how she was laying in bed, she began to cry and she hollered, "You *did* see me!"

Kelly went on to say, "When I woke up this morning, I couldn't believe I was lying on my stomach. I haven't lain on my stomach for a long, long time. My stomach has been so swollen and sore that I couldn't lay on it, but last night I did because when I woke up, my hands were stuck together where my cheek rested on them.

"I must not have moved a muscle all night long. My hands were so badly asleep that I didn't think I was going to get them apart."

I backed away from her and looked. Her stomach wasn't swollen at all. She was still very thin, like a walking skeleton – but with bright, shining eyes, long beautiful hair and the biggest smile I have ever seen. Kelly was definitely healed and ready to re-enter life.

Later on that same day, I received a phone call from Kelly. She was crying hysterically.

When she finally got calmed down, she said, "The Doctors still think I am going to die! I thought Jesus healed me! Did He heal me or didn't He?"

I said, "Hang on, Kelly. I'll be up to see you in a few minutes."

Immediately I went to work, looking up every Scripture I could find about trusting in God, not in man. I listed them on a yellow legal tablet.

> *"Commit your way to the Lord; trust in Him and He will do this."* (Psalm 37:5 NIV)

> *"It is better to take refuge in the Lord than to trust in man."* (Psalm 118:8 NIV)

> *"Trust in the Lord with all your heart and lean not on your own understanding."* (Proverbs 3:5 NIV)

> *"It is better to take refuge in the Lord than to trust in princes."* (Psalm 118:9 NIV)

> *"Stop trusting in man, who has but a breath in his nostrils. Of what account is he?"*

(Isaiah 2:22 NIV)

"This is what the Lord says: 'Cursed is the one, who trusts in man, Who depends on flesh for his strength and whose heart turns away from the Lord.'"
(Jeremiah 17:5 NIV)

And on and on I went, listing every Scripture I could find, hoping to convince Kelly that God does things that science cannot understand or figure out.

I knew I didn't have to show Kelly Scriptures to prove to her that God heals. She had physical proof that something dynamic and divine had happened to her. She had a spiritual and physical encounter of a divine kind with the Master Healer Jesus of Nazareth.

But if the devil could put enough pressure on her through those she would naturally trust – namely, her doctors – then it was possible for her healing to be reversed by her fear.

Remember Mark 11:23.

"And does not doubt in his heart, but believes that those things he says will be done, he will have whatever he says."

I had to help her recognize that the circumstances of this physical life were the culprits. Though they may appear to be true, they are, in fact, lies – because of the ignorance that plagues humankind due to disbelief in God's power.

When I got to the hospital, I made Kelly read each Scripture two or three times and then I made her explain what they meant to her. By the time we got through the entire list, Kelly was convinced that the doctors were wrong. She was willing to give God the benefit of the doubt and watch and wait.

By the end of the day Kelly had created quite a stir in the eating disorder ward, and had no doubt caused much incredulous discussion in the conference rooms as well.

Kelly was not shy about telling everyone that Jesus had healed her. She maintained that testimony and was very vocal about it. So vocal, in fact, that the nurses and her doctor came to her and told her to not tell anyone until they were sure.

What was going to convince them? When Kelly began to function totally on her own again – when she resumed a normal appetite and her bodily functions returned to normal – then and only then would they be sure of a true miracle.

During her first day she began to eat any food she could find. By the next afternoon, things began to move. I never thought I would ever see anyone so excited about having a bowel movement.

Once her kidneys and bladder began to work, the doctors said, "Remember, don't put so much faith on this divine healing stuff. Your womb has been eaten up and your stomach may still fail you."

Later on that week, everything was working fine in Kelly's formerly battered body.

She was dismissed from the hospital exactly four weeks from the day she received the Lord Jesus Christ as her personal Savior.

The last word from the doctors was to not be surprised if she could never have children. They believed her ovaries were still damaged and would never allow her to get pregnant.

Would the bad news never end?

One year later I counseled Kelly and her fiancé for marriage and performed their wedding. One year later, two years from her discharge from the hospital, I received a birth announcement and a picture of Kelly's beautiful new baby daughter.

By the way, Kelly never used, or desired, cocaine again. She was truly delivered and healed by the divine hand of a loving and giving Heavenly Father.

That didn't end God's plan for that eating disorder ward however!

One night toward the end of her stay, I went to the hospital to visit Kelly and the medical staff had been testing her all day. They had her in a conference room when I got there, asking her questions.

The nurses wouldn't let me go to her room and they seemed very cold and rude for some reason, but they were also very busy tending to other patients.

It was late. I had been through a tough day and I was a bit nervous about the nurse's attitude that night, which was totally unlike any of the other nights I had visited Kelly.

I felt very uneasy even being there, and because there were no waiting rooms in the eating disorder ward, and the common room was being used by a group therapy session, I just sat on the floor in the hall, waiting for Kelly to come out.

I pulled up my knees, wrapped my arms around them and put my head down to pray quietly in the Spirit. Great peace came over me. I seemed to doze off for a second or two.

Suddenly, I became aware that someone was looking at me. I opened my eyes and saw five pairs of slipper-clad feet standing around me in the hall.

I looked up and there were five young ladies, all of them patients undergoing treatment for the same kinds of problems as Kelly.

One of them spoke up when I raised my head and asked, "Are you Kelly's preacher?"

I said, "Yes, I guess I am. What can I do for you?"

The one that started the conversation went on to say, "Can we ask you some questions?" Without waiting for my answer she said, "What happened to Kelly?"

"God healed her," I answered.

One of the others said, "Will He do that for *us?*"

What an opportunity! What a question!

"Sure!" I said. "If you are willing to pay the same price Kelly paid." I went ahead and explained that Kelly had asked Jesus to be her Savior and God had healed her!

"How do we do that?" asked another.

"I did that once in my home church" another one said. "But it sure hasn't done me much good lately."

I told her that just maybe it was because she hadn't paid Him much attention lately, and she shook her head, disgusted with herself, in agreement.

At that I asked them if there was some place we could talk, or at least somewhere where we could all get on the same physical level. My tail bone was numb from sitting on the floor and I was terribly uncomfortable getting the fifth degree from five young ladies while I was only able to look up their noses.

I truly enjoy sharing the Gospel with people but I would much rather look someone in the eye than up their noses.

One of them said, "Sure, let's all go to my room."

So off we went, and I began to explain the Gospel of Jesus Christ to them. I shared with them that we are all sinners and therefore we have all fallen far short of God's expectations (Romans 6:23).

I told them that to invite Jesus into their hearts meant that they had to repent, turn from their sin and ask God to forgive them and deliver them from their self-centeredness.

To make a longer story shorter, five young ladies bowed their heads that night and surrendered their hearts to the Lord Jesus.

I knew that their salvation was for real. I then explained to them that along with salvation comes all that God is.

"Is God sick?" I asked. "Is God hooked on drugs? Is God hooked on bad habits of any kind?"

And of course the answer is no, and they knew it. So then we began to praise God for their healing and their deliverance. We subsequently had quite a raucous time in that room that night!

In fact, we were having so much fun that a nurse came in to see what all the commotion was about.

When I explained that I had prayed with them for their salvation and we were just thanking God for healing them, she became visibly upset and said, "We'll see about that!" and turned on her heals to charge haughtily out of the room.

The following day, I received another phone call from the hospital. The head nurse from the eating disorder ward called to let me know that I was not welcome back on her floor unless they had my name on a request sheet from one of their patients.

She said now that Kelly was discharged, I had no further business there. And then she hung up without giving me any chance to speak or ask her questions.

God had a way of getting me into that place and He had a very convincing way of informing me that my work there was completed – for now, anyway.

The next week I followed up on the five young ladies. Kelly helped me with their names and after researching I finally got in touch with one of them.

The good news was that they were all discharged from the hospital days after I met them and they met Jesus!

I can't help but believe that they were all healed and delivered as well.

"Oh, give thanks to the Lord, for He is good! For His mercy endures forever."
(1 Chronicles 16:34 KJV)

Chapter 9
South Of The Border

In 1986, three men from my church and I took a missions trip deep into the interior of Mexico.

We took in 20 pairs of new shoes to distribute as the needs presented themselves; our intentions were to bless pastors with the gift of new shoes.

Our basic reason for the trip was to help do some building at an orphanage in Nuevo Padilla and to encourage some of the native pastors.

We borrowed a motor home, but – alas – the engine blew up a few miles outside of Laredo, Texas.

The phone book provided us a name of a Mexican mission's effort based in Laredo. I shared our dilemma with them and they immediately invited us over to their office to check us out.

After talking to them for a while, sharing the details of our mission's trip, the head man offered us a 15-passenger van if we would deliver some papers for him to their office in Saltillo, Mexico.

There were some Mexican pastors in the mountains near Monterey who just happened to be in the Saltillo area, so we took their van and papers and prepared to leave for the border.

While at our first stop in Nuevo Padilla, we encountered a young boy who had almost cut his right thumb off by falling down on a machete.

The wound was rancid with infection and wrapped in a dirty rag. We also noticed he had no shoes, which was common to that area of cardboard shanties, bathing in the not-so-nearby river and eating under unsanitary conditions.

We prayed for his hand and all we had to disinfect it with was a bottle of Clorox. We were so afraid it would hurt badly enough that it would scare him off and he would not come back.

Because he needed to come back to have the bandage changed, we decided to have the interpreter offer him a new pair of shoes if he came back the next day.

We poured on the Clorox, but there was no reaction at all. After we cleaned up his wound we realized this thumb was in a bad way and serious infection had set in.

We prayed again, applied some antibiotic cream from the van's first aid kit, wrapped it in a clean bandage and let him go with the promise he would return the following day.

We were no doctors, but we knew if we didn't help him get rid of the infection he would probably die of gangrene or infection in his blood.

The next day he showed up first thing in the morning with about 50 other people of all ages.

They were not as interested in his cut thumb as they were of the promise of *neuvo zapatos* (new shoes) but we did not know about their true motivation until after we treated the boy's thumb, which was no worse, but neither was it any better.

After we rewrapped his hand he asked, "*Zapatos?*" and we knew exactly what he wanted. At that moment the people lined up behind him.

We only had 20 pairs of leather dress shoes and we knew we had a few tennis shoes for children. But there were more kids than 20 and the crowd was continuing to grow.

We opened the back door of the van and reached for a box of shoes and, miraculously, we got the exact size the first try. Joy and happiness lit up his face and the crowd went wild as the boy paraded around showing off his new shoes.

Suddenly we noticed they were looking to us as they began lining up behind the van. I don't mind admitting that a little fear spread over all four of us as we looked at each other with the unspoken question of, "*Now* what do we do?"

We finally decided that there was definitely a need for shoes in this town. And all we could do was to hand out what we had until they ran out. At least there would be 20 happy people and that would have helped out somewhat, we hoped.

The next person came up, barefoot, with big brown eyes pleading with us for shoes without saying a word. We got a pail of water and the missionary there got us some towels and we washed his feet, dried them and reached for a box of shoes and – *voila!* – the exact size again.

The next person sidled up and we repeated the same steps. As we washed their feet we pleaded with God to provide shoes that would fit this person. There's nothing worse than a person with clean feet and no shoes after they had witnessed all those in front of them receiving a brand new pair of shoes that fit perfectly.

This went on all day long. At one point, we noticed that the line was getting longer rather than shorter and we were afraid to look at the dwindling stock-pile in the back of the van.

However, every time we reached for a box of shoes we had the perfect fit and type for the person standing there with clean feet, looking at us with those hopeful, big brown eyes.

By the end of that day we had given out hundreds of pairs of shoes from the stock of 20 pairs we had in the van!

How did that happen?

Remember the loaves and fishes that God multiplied in Matthew 14:13-21 and John 6:1-14? Well, He also multiplied new shoes that day in Mexico; but that's not all.

The last day we were in Nuevo Padilla, we were going to change the little boy's thumb bandage for the last time and leave some antibiotic cream and bandages with him and instructions for changing it daily.

When we took the bandage off his hand we were looking at a perfectly healed hand with no scar or a trace that there had even been an injury.

Another miracle? Unequivocally, absolutely and undeniably!

That was our main subject of conversation as we journeyed on to our next destination – Pastor Peppi's home and church in the mountains near Monterrey.

As we talked about all we had just witnessed, we began to wonder if we were dreaming when it came to the young boy's hand. The only difference between his right and left hand was the right hand was clean because of his bandage. Other than that you could see nothing that even resembled a hand that almost lost the thumb.

We finally reached Pastor Peppi's home after traveling seemingly endless miles over the rough Mexican highways, creeping over mountain roads and finally making the last hundred yards on foot.

Pastor Peppi was a happy-go-lucky young pastor who had two very small boys, a young daughter in her teens and a very accommodating wife who endeavored to make us all very comfortable in her home.

In fact, she and Peppi gave up their bed for their guests. I wasn't too crazy about sleeping with my traveling partners, but, when in Rome…

The first night we were there, one of the guys with us noticed that Peppi had no shoes, nor did his wife and one little boy;

the other little boy of about 10 had old tire tread tied to each foot like flip-flops.

A fellow named Jerry, the youngest Christian in the group said, "Man, I wish we could give this family some shoes! I'm going to the van to look – just in case we missed a box or two."

"Are you kidding me?" I cried. "We just gave away more shoes than we brought! How could we have missed anything?"

Jerry said, "I'm going down to the van just in case. Do you have a flashlight?"

"There's no flashlight here, so I'll go with you to carry back the load and keep you from getting lost," I said laughingly.

Have you ever been in Mexico or any third-world country where they have no street lights? It's dark! If the moon isn't out it's so dark you can't see your hand right in front of you.

We did have a sliver of moonlight, but it was still very dark and we tripped and stumbled like a couple blind men.

Jerry opened the back door of the van and exclaimed excitedly, "Come here, Larry. I need your help!"

I was looking for a flashlight up front, but I immediately went to the back of the van to help Jerry. I thought he had fallen down or something.

As soon as I got there he said, "Take these." He then put two boxes in my hands. I said, "What are these?" and Jerry replied, "Looks like shoe boxes to me!"

I returned to see if I could find a flashlight and to secretly look inside the boxes to see what we had. I found one and looked inside and there were two pairs of adult shoes – one set of wing-tips for men and a nice pair for a lady.

Just then Jerry shut the back door and came to the front with three more.

"You have got to be kidding me!" I exclaimed in disbelief.

"Nope! I'm not kidding. And I'll bet these boxes fit these kids," he stated matter-of-factly.

We couldn't wait to get back to the house so we outright flew over the rocks and jumped the holes that just moments before we had been stumbling over and falling into.

When we got to the house, everybody had a new pair of shoes. But Pastor Peppi's would not fit his feet; they were too tight and he barely got his foot into them.

Jerry took back one of the shoes, reached down inside to pull out a pair of men's dress socks and gave it back to Peppi. He took the other shoe and found a pair of socks in it as well.

Well, you guessed it; Peppi received a new pair of well-fitting wing-tip shoes with two new pairs of socks. The kids all got new tennis shoes. The teenage daughter and mom each received a nice pair of ladies flats that were very dressy.

Talk about a happy family! Nothing beat their joy except our knowing that God has been with us, meeting the need of every person we encountered.

What powerful excitement and wonderment! We couldn't stop talking about what we witnessed. We were in awe.

Intriguingly, the only man I have lost track of over the ensuing years is Jerry – the youngest Christian and newest member of our group.

As I write this, I remember that I was privileged to lead Jerry to the Lord only a few months before our trip and I lost track of him less than a year after we returned.

Could he have been an angel of the Lord? Maybe there was more of a miracle working for us and with us than any of us will ever know this side of Heaven.

Chapter 10
Hungry For God

*F*or the next six years I would remain the lead pastor of that lovely little country church in southern Iowa.

This was to be my seminary experience as Holy Spirit worked *on* me as well as *through* me to take this unknown enclave from a weekly attendance of 35 (men, women and children) to a regular attendance of over a 100 plus their children, which was full capacity.

It wasn't long before Holy Spirit brought me a musically talented young man who quickly became my best friend. He played bass and sang beautifully. I had never heard someone play bass and sing lead. He was, and is, an awesome musician.

This was back in the day when the only acceptable form of worship was an organ and a piano, and only hymnals contained what were deemed acceptable songs.

It didn't take long before I recognized his talent and then we began experimenting with church services by bringing in a few contemporary choruses to replace the weekly hymns.

This did three important things in the church; it caused Holy Spirit to move on people, and it riled up some of the original members. But it excited the younger crowd which, at that time, far outnumbered the old-timers.

The word spread around the county that there was a new pastor at this little country church and things were hopping over there.

The crowd increased weekly and the Holy Spirit brought us another young couple; he played drums and his wife played the keyboard and sang like an angel in cowboy boots.

That's when our Sunday services really began to change; much to the fear, chagrin and dismay of many.

All I knew was that I wanted God and all He could bring us. I had no idea what that would look like in a church service, but I knew I needed Him because I didn't know what to do but to cry out to Him.

I reminded Him of the promise He had made me just a short four years earlier: "Trust Me, and I will show you things the educated can only dream about."

I had also asked Holy Spirit for a favor when He called me into ministry and I agreed to follow Him into ministry. I asked Him to keep me on the *cutting edge* of what He is doing on the earth.

I began to spend Friday evenings and Saturdays pacing the floor of the church praying in tongues, worshiping God and asking Him to move mightily in our church services.

One Friday evening our bass player showed up and we prayed the entire night through, seeking God for His power and presence in our church services.

It became a weekly tradition that my friend and I would spend Friday nights praying at the church. Others would join us occasionally, coming and going, but we were there without fail every week.

We began meeting Thursday nights for music practice and we would stay late into the night after practice, just seeking God. We turned the overhead lights off and allowed the alter lights to be our only source of light. It was, in a word, awesome. We wondered.

"What if God shows up?"

It happened one Thursday night when the music group was practicing for Sunday's service. Our worship leader insisted we get some harmony in the singing of our choruses.

We sang the same chorus over and over for over a half hour before it began to sound exceedingly sweet.

I was singing with my eyes closed trying to get my harmony part just right when all of a sudden one of the girls standing next to me fell on her face with a triumphant thump.

For some reason we didn't quit singing and I inwardly hoped she wasn't dead. But no one stopped singing, and she seemed to be, despite her collapse, alright.

There was suddenly electricity in the air and it was like we were all holding our breath, if that's possible, while singing. She just lay there, not moving. We kept singing and singing, and there she lay.

Suddenly she rolled over and sat up.

We stopped singing and helped her to a chair when she said, "I saw Jesus and He told me to keep in mind that this is only practice, but to be aware that He heard our prayers.

"He said He is going to make Himself known to everyone in the church, but we have to remain faithful to Him and to be ready to help the church host His presence."

The following Sunday we were packed with standing room only.

A young lady raised her hand and asked if I believe in the laying on of hands for healing.

I said, "Yes, indeed!"

She stood up and explained that she and her husband had been trying for years to have a baby. She was currently several months pregnant but, she said, "This past week the doctor noticed a growth on my ovaries the size of an orange. He told me that it could be taken out, which he recommended. But he was very certain that during the surgery the baby wouldn't survive the operation."

It got worse as she continued, "He also said that if I do nothing he's afraid the growth would eventually kill the baby as fast as it is growing."

Her request was for me to lay hands on her and pray for a miracle. I couldn't very well say no, but I wasn't as sure as she was that my prayers could be that powerful. I know I began to sweat as she came down the aisle.

She stood in the middle aisle and I was on a raised platform, so I approached her and, in fear, simply and tremblingly laid my hands on her shoulders and said, "Jesus, You've got to heal this woman. Amen!"

Bam! Down she went with a thud.

And there she lay. That was it? I said "amen," so it must be! My mind was buzzing. I wanted to look like I knew what was going on, but I didn't. Did I kill her? Why did she fall down?

I turned and went to the pulpit and started the message as I kept one eye on the woman for some sign of life; a twitch, a sigh – or anything, Lord!

I am sure my message was awful that morning because I couldn't keep my mind on what I wanted to impart to the congregation. I could tell people in the audience were thinking, "Is that *it*? He said 'amen,' so it must be!"

About midway through the message the young woman quietly got up and slid into a seat close to her husband. I breathed a sigh of relief, and then I preached up a storm.

Two weeks later she returned to church and wanted to give testimony.

"Last week," she began. "I had another ultra-sound and the doctor said the baby is doing splendidly and the growth is totally gone!"

She continued, "The doctor apologized for scaring me and said it must have been an irregularity in the machine or that he misread the report. He wasn't sure, but he was sorry just the same.

"I told him Jesus healed me, and that his eyes and the machine were just fine."

A few months later she gave birth to a beautiful baby girl and we dedicated her joyously to the Lord.

One Saturday the music team and I went to a Hill Song Praise and Worship Seminar in Des Moines. During the Q & A session, a question was raised by one of the teams from a much larger church.

"What happens when He shows up in church? What do you do then?"

At that moment I knew He had me on the *cutting edge,* because He had already shown up in our church many times by then.

During my six years there, we got rid of the out houses, installed indoors bathrooms, added a modern kitchen, waterproofed the basement that flooded every year, got new pews to increase our capacity to 140, built rooms for the youth and added two offices and some classroom space for the children.

We ran an annual, week-long vacation bible school and had over 100 children in attendance for the week with a big program on the Friday evening.

It must be noted that all this happened in spite of a hostile response from the original folks, all 20 of them. The remaining 120 wanted all God could bring us. But there was a constant undercurrent which made for some special challenges for me and my family.

At the last annual business meeting the original 20 tried their best to have me fired. But it was too late, as God had saved, healed and changed all the new folks. So they fought in vain which increased their hostility.

In 1991 God directed me to resign my secular job – a 27-year, highly paid career in computer systems analysis and design – and began ministering full time with no immediate promise of a salary.

I honestly don't know how we made it, except to say it was all God's doing; we were never in need of anything and somehow all our bills got paid in full.

We were so excited about what God was doing that nothing else mattered. He promised the day I called on Him that if I would seek the Kingdom of God and His righteousness, all I would ever need would be awarded me (Matthew 6:33).

He meant it. He was, and remains, always faithful to us as we continued seeking Him.

Chapter 11
Forgiven, Forgiven, Forgiven

*D*uring the mid to late '70s, through the mid 80's, our nation's economy was taking a nose dive led by runaway inflation and who knows what all else.

I am not an economist, so I don't pretend to understand why this happened. All I know is I was fighting for my financial life to keep from having to file bankruptcy.

To complicate this financial dilemma I had, less than a year prior to this time I had gotten fired from a very well-paying job.

Looking back on this time period I can see that I was still suffering from the shock and humiliation of being fired. Along with working long and hard hours as a farmer trying to eke out a living from the small parcel of land, it was becoming very clear that my dreams were dying. I was failing!

This was the tremendous pressure I was living under when I came to know Jesus Christ as my personal Savior.

The Lord took me through all the humiliation of having an equipment auction to help me pay past-due debt and taxes. It wasn't easy, but He walked me through it, giving me comfort and strength when and where I needed – steadily, constantly, hourly.

The Holy Spirit proved He was interested in every little aspect of my life as He worked me through one of the most painfully stressful experiences I had ever encountered.

After selling all my possessions, moving out of our new home (that was stolen from us), plus pastoring our first little country church, we ended with a small piece of land I was purchasing from my father on a personal contract. I also had over $60,000 of unsecured operating capital and miscellaneous debt I owed a local bank who was trying to keep me out of bankruptcy court.

The interest rates on the operating capital and unsecured debt had skyrocketed during the last of the Carter years from six per cent to a peak of 21 per cent; which is where it was in this part of my saga.

I finally secured a good job again, being rehired by a company I had worked for a decade prior. I once again felt better about myself and life seemed like it was going to get a bit better.

Getting rehired was a part of this miracle. I was trying to sell a men's clothing store new lights over the men's suites when a lens popped out of my glasses, hit the marble floor and smashed.

It was no longer a single lens but the million pieces of what was a lens.

As I fumbled with the sale, an old boss of mine happened to be trying on a suit when he spotted me.

"Larry Low! What in the world are you doing?" he asked.

"Trying to hide from you," I wanted to say, but instead I said, "Trying to see you. I just broke my lens." As he reached out his hand and shook mine.

"Yeah, I see that!" he replied as he continued, "No, I mean what you are doing for a job these days?"

Before I could respond, he continued, "Listen, how would you like to come to work for me again?"

I just about fell right over.

How would I like to go back to my professional career that I had over 18 years of my life, and give up selling light bulbs? I almost climbed over a rack of suits to kiss him, "Where do you want me to sign?"

It was less than a month before Christmas, we were not making it financially and Holy Spirit said through my ex-boss, "Can you come to work for me next Monday?"

I was on the verge of tears as I excitedly and emphatically responded, "You can surely bet I would!"

He said, "Good, I will see you Monday. Have a great weekend."

Next thing, I excused myself and went home to celebrate with Dixie. It looked like things might be turning around.

When Dixie asked, "How much did they offer?" I didn't have a clue. All I knew was they wanted me back. And I was tired of selling light bulbs.

The job, as it turned out, was wonderful. My boss saw to it that I received the same bonus as other employees for Christmas, making Christmas that year very merry.

But I still had financial problems that were eating us up. I was eyeball deep in debt and I hadn't even been making utility money running all over trying to light up the state.

Reality said we would never see the light of day financially (no pun intended) unless we had a major miracle.

I had reasoned that if I could sell the small piece (65 acres) of land, I might just be able to pay off the bank debt and then work on the contract note that I owed my dad.

The problem was, I had to ask my dad to allow me to sell *his* land to pay off *my* debt at the bank.

Dad didn't hesitate when I asked him. He said, "Do what you need to do, Larry. I trust you. Things are going to get better. So keep your chin up, son."

No one in their right mind would have done what my dad did for me. I made up my mind right then that I would never miss a payment to him and I would pay it off in full if I had to work the rest of my life to do it.

I had it listed through a local realtor plus the banker knew I had it for sale. The asking price was $75,000 – priced to sell so I could pay off the bank and my dad.

Every month we wrote a $150 check to pay my dad and $600 for the bank. The only trouble was the bank's interest was more than what I was paying. I was literally losing ground with each payment.

One day while I was working I received a phone call from the banker. He said; "We have a buyer for the land. The price isn't where you want it but we are prepared to make you an offer."

"I'm listening," I said as new hope surged through my heart. In an instant I began to visualize life without debt and maybe, a little extra left over for us.

The banker continued with, "The offer is only 15 thousand…"

I almost blacked out. I was feeling physically sick as I heard those words. I didn't hear anything else. My mind was calculating 6 minus 15 thousand minus the seven per cent realtor fee would leave me over 40 thousand plus what I still owed the bank, not to mention the balance I still owed my dad.

I couldn't speak. I wanted to cry. I fought back the tears.

Suddenly I heard the caller say, "Are you there Larry? Are you okay?"

Angrily I replied, "Are you kidding me? Fifteen thousand isn't enough to do me any good at all!"

I was crying, angry in disbelief with at least a dozen other emotions trying to take me down.

Suddenly my mind cleared just enough for me to hear, "...and if you take the offer we will take care of the remainder of your debt."

"What do you mean you will take care of my debt?" I asked the banker, incredulous.

"We will write it off," He said.

I said in a doubtful tone, "Did you say that you, the bank, will write off my debt if I take an offer that is way too small to pay off much of anything?"

"That's exactly what I am saying," he replied, while I sat in stunned disbelief. "To do this, I will need you to come to the bank to sign the papers today. Is that possible? We really want to get this thing wrapped up and I am sure you would like that as well. Can you come over today?"

I still can't believe my response. I said, "Uh, um, I don't know. Let me call you back." Click. I hung up the phone without even waiting for his response.

I immediately called my wife. "Dixie, I just got a call from the bank and they sold our land for us but sit down before I tell you the price; 15 thousand."

"And then how much a month?" she said, thinking that was the down payment with contract terms to follow.

"That's it." I said. "But there's more."

Dixie was upset to say the least and she let me know it. "That's not enough to do us or your dad any good!" she said emphatically.

"I know, I know. But there's more, I'm telling you. The banker said that if we take this offer they will write off all our debt. I think they said *all* our debt. Yeah, I am sure they said *all* our debt. What should I do?"

My mind was still swirling with emotion and fear that I had misunderstood the offer.

"I'm going to the bank right now," I said without even waiting for my wife's response.

I hung up the phone, told my boss I had an emergency to tend to and would tell him all about it when I returned, and immediately left work.

I was so nervous I could barely insert my car key into the door lock. Finally I got in my car, started it and somehow got to the bank.

When I pulled into the parking space I couldn't believe my eyes – my wife was there!

We asked to see the banker who called me and was asked to sit in the waiting area until he was able to take us. All I could think of was how rude I had been to him on the phone and prayed that the Lord would smooth things over for me and prepare me for the news, good or bad.

It seemed like I sat there for days, when in fact it was only a few minutes, and then I was greeted by the loan officer himself sporting a big, benevolent smile.

I thought my eyes were playing tricks on me as Dixie and I looked at each other in disbelief as we were greeted by the same man who foreclosed on us from the defunct Federal Land Bank only a few years before.

Suddenly I was met with a rush of fear when he said; "You can't believe how happy I am to see you both. Our last meeting was less than desirable for all concerned."

Now, in a very cheerful tone, almost giddy with excitement he said again, "I am so glad you could make it this quickly. I have what I think is great news for you; I hope you think so too. Please come in and let me run this thing by you again."

L. F. Low

Before me, on his desk, were three note contracts which all totaled $55,000, including interest, to that very moment in time.

I had been in meetings like this before, where the bank was demanding payment on the notes laid out on the desk and as I looked at these three I began to feel sick.

The loan officer, sensing how I was feeling, jumped right in with "Now don't go jumping to conclusions, Larry! I think I know what you are feeling and thinking and again, I want you to know I am so happy to be the one doing this after our last meeting."

And he continued "We are prepared to offer you *total forgiveness* for all your debt with us if you sign this sale agreement with our buyer. Plus..." (and it was an emphatic and excited plus when he continued), "*Plus*, we worked a deal with the realtor to waive their usual commission and fees so we will be doing all the paper work.

"The reason I needed you here today was because of the realtor's deadline – also, we wanted to get this all wrapped up for you."

I sat there, again, in stunned disbelief, tears running down my cheeks, unable to say a word, knowing that if I opened my mouth to say anything I would burst into a full-fledged bawling fit.

After a few awkward seconds, which seemed more like hours, I asked, "Why?"

Then I burst into tears.

I apologized, blew my nose and cleared my throat as Dixie said what I tried to say, "Why are you doing this? Are you doing this for other farmers as well?"

The loan officer said, "All I know is that this morning, during our weekly loan officers meeting, the president of the bank spread these notes out on the conference table and said, 'Let's work to make this deal so everyone wins here. If Larry accepts the offer to buy, forgive these debts. If he doesn't, have his head examined,'" he said with a chuckle.

My response was, "Where do I sign."

As I signed the offer to buy and the realtor's paperwork waiving their fees, the loan officer was stamping in big red letters, "forgiven, forgiven, forgiven" across the face of each note; forgiving me of over $55,000.

We continued paying my father for his land that I sold until I paid off every penny. The day I gave my dad the last payment he said, "Now I have a surprise for you."

He got his check book and wrote me a check for every last penny of interest I had paid him since I signed the contract with him several years prior.

I couldn't believe it! But on the other hand, that was just like him. After all, he was my dad, a fine, fine man.

Thank You Jesus! Two huge acts of the Holy Spirit *for* this regular guy!

***

We were still serving the little country church as their pastor. In my eyes, good things were happening; people were getting saved on a regular basis, I had witnessed many miracles and the Lord had found us a home and moved us into it, giving us a home we could call ours once again.

Things were looking up – with one not so small exception.

One evening we came home from church and there was a car parked in the shadows, directly out in front of our home.

"Who's that?" Dixie asked.

"I don't know, but I'm going to find out," I replied with some force.

I didn't recognize the car. I told Dixie to take the girls inside. I walked toward the car.

When I got within 20 feet of the car, the driver rolled down his passenger side window.

"Can I help you?" I inquired.

"You sure can!" was the sure response from the man behind the wheel.

"How can I help you? What do you want? Do I know you?" I asked.

His response was directly out of a cheesy detective movie with added profanities.

He said, "You are going to get to know me a lot better if you don't quit preaching that insane bulls--t message you are preaching out at the church."

In shock I said, "What message is that?"

"That Jesus bulls--t," he said. "Knock it off or you will wish you had. I'm serious. I know where you live."

And then he squealed off before I could press him further to identify himself.

Praise God! I had actually been threatened for preaching the Gospel of Jesus Christ!

How cool! Things were looking up until...

One Friday I was scheduled to be gone and I happened to return home early to uncover a sinister prayer meeting in the basement of our little church.

As I drove up to the church, I was shocked to find the parking lot filled with unfamiliar cars.

I opened the walk-in door to the basement, thinking I would go in the back way and not disturb what I assumed to be going on upstairs in the sanctuary.

As I opened the door I was met with candles burning, lights off, and people gathered in a circle – caterwauling like a gathering of devil worshipers!

I turned on the lights and I don't know who was more surprised; them or me. I ordered everyone to leave. I was shocked to see familiar faces in that group. They all left without saying a word.

I went upstairs and found a bunch of strangers in the sanctuary doing the same thing. I was so incensed I was spitting nails as I ordered them all to leave.

With all unwanted "visitors" gone, I sat in the sanctuary, too shook-up to drive.

"What just happened?" I thought. "God, what am I doing wrong?" I shouted.

But all was quiet; I received no response. I began to feel like someone was watching me as chills ran down my spine. God had always answered me before, so why the silence now?

I suddenly became more fearful of no response from the Lord than I did about the threat, the devilish prayer meeting and the feeling of someone watching.

The following Saturday was hell as I tried to clear my mind and get a message that made sense without anger, suspicion or fear.

The Sundays that followed were no better. It was hard to preach. I felt somehow detached. To me, nothing made sense anymore.

Many in the congregation recognized something was going on and one Sunday after church several of them cornered me in my office with their questions.

I didn't tell them about the threat in front of my house because I didn't know – but what it might have been one of those standing before me. I did, however, tell them about the "prayer meeting" I broke up several weeks prior to this.

One man said matter-of-factly, "Sounds like the devil don't want you here anymore! So what are you going to do about it?"

Good question. What could I do about it but pray. And pray I did, with great passion. Hearing from the Lord became exceptionally difficult all of a sudden.

* * *

One sunny and bright Monday morning, after a horrible Sunday night's experience with the congregation's response to a musical group we invited to minister to us, I sat in front of the church building and said, "God, I don't believe 1 John 4:4 anymore.

I don't believe that "greater is He that is in me than he that is in the world." It feels to me like the devil is winning. I don't hear from You anymore and I don't know what I did wrong! What is going on?"

And the Lord spoke clearly by saying, "I have left this church! *Ichabod* was written on the wall weeks ago!"

I then began recalling some strange incidents that were out of the ordinary; mostly in the way certain people responded to me.

At the time, I compared those little incidents to what God had been doing and they were not hard to overlook. I felt I just needed to be the bigger one, the mature one. You know, bear my cross and crucify my earthly desire to get even or put them in their place.

God said emphatically, "I am no longer here. Those that own this building no longer want me, so I left. Follow Me and trust Me."

At that moment I realized that the Holy Spirit can be grieved to the point that He will back away. I hated the place without Holy Spirit's presence in it.

Everything became laborious. The people all seemed to be doing everything they could to destroy me and discourage my family.

I never knew until that moment, and after the little investigation I did following it, that the building we were in was not owned by the church, but by the owners of the farm on which it sat.

Needless to say, the owners were not friendly toward God and likely felt that we were creating entirely too much traffic on that gravel road.

The following Sunday I resigned my position and left the church. The Lord instructed me to follow Ezekiel 12:1-16. Suddenly, quietly, strangely excited, I walked out of that church, never to return.

If God wasn't there, I wasn't going to stay! I followed Him.

This ended my adventure in my first church but this was only a quick glance at what Holy Spirit did during my first few years of that ministry.

I didn't tell about the time He told me to pull over as I drove toward home one night and there I sat, on a dark country road, inside my car in His glorious light as He told me about what my future held and how I would serve Him.

About that time He spoke through me about trouble and death unless the one I was talking to also turned and repented – he didn't and he died sometime later just as the Lord had said he would.

Or how a woman in that church got saved and her husband subsequently gave us the house we were living in.

Or how my second church began, or how we acquired the land on which to build our beautiful new building.

Little did I know that when I left that little country church my adventure was only just beginning!

Chapter 12
God Guides And Provides

"And I will meet all your needs in accordance with My riches in Glory by Christ Jesus."
(Philippians 4:19)

Life became exceptionally exciting once we made the decision to follow the Lord and stepped away from the old church.

I still had some debt, though, but God lead me to resign my career of 27 years in the computer system development industry. So there I sat with a family, a home with the usual expenses.

My middle daughter was getting married, my youngest daughter was in high school and now we were at a new church with a handful of eager believers.

But we had no understanding of what to do next, and no income to speak of.

I don't know what most folks would do in a situation like this, but I will say what Dixie and I did; we prayed and sought God's plan and followed His instructions exactly.

We didn't seek out any of those in the church. We didn't tell anyone what we were going to do because we had no idea. And, as a matter of course, we prayed – hard.

On Sundays, Dixie and I would go to one of the many county parks close by where we would walk through the timber, pray and seek directions from the Lord.

During the week I prayed, began a radio ministry, prayed, recorded and edited messages, prayed and prayed some more.

This went on for several weeks and neither one of us heard anything from the Lord as far as definite steps of action. I continued to hear, "Trust Me son, trust Me," and the words, "new life."

I didn't tell anyone what the Lord was saying because I didn't fully understand anything, except that He wanted me to trust Him about new life.

One Sunday evening we returned home from our day in the park and when we turned the corner onto the street where we lived, it was filled with cars.

Dixie and I looked at each other in disbelief because this was a small, quiet farm town and it was quite rare that there were cars on the street anywhere late Sunday evenings.

It soon became obvious that people were in our house.

As soon as we opened the front door one of my daughters met us to explain, "Dad! All these people want you and mom to be their pastor! I didn't know what else to do because they wanted to make sure they could speak to you as a group. Hope you don't mind. I just didn't know what else to do!"

I reassured her that it was okay and said, "Let's go see what they want."

They all gave us their reasons why they wanted me, but the one I listened to the longest said, "I asked God what to do, and He said to come see you."

I said, "Well let's all ask God what He wants us to do. Then we'll all share what God is saying to us."

We immediately went into prayer and during the opening of our prayer my home phone rang. My middle daughter answered it and I heard her say, "Well, he's in prayer right now. But I will tell him when they've finished. What's your number? Thank you, Mike. I'll tell him. Good-bye."

Not too long after that we said, "Speak to us Lord. We need Your direction. Amen!"

My daughter immediately said, "Dad, Mike A. called you and he is at the airport in Boston. He wants you to call him right now."

Mike A. was an evangelist friend of mine who I hadn't seen for several weeks as he was traveling.

"Hey Mike, what's happening?" I asked as he answered the phone.

He said, "Brother Larry! I've only got a couple of seconds so listen carefully. As we were landing here in Boston the Lord said, 'Call Larry and tell him that when the world was dark and confusion was over the whole earth I didn't quit; I said *let there be* and new life sprang forth.' Do you have any idea what that means?"

"Yep, I think I know what He means," I said. "Thanks for calling, brother. Look me up next time you are in our area." He assured me he would and then I hung up the phone.

I said, "It looks like the Lord wants a new church here as well and He obviously wants it called something to do with 'new life.'"

We started our new church by holding bible studies at home on Wednesday evenings, and meetings that night in the homes of one in attendance at our Sunday services.

Hence, New Life Church sprang forth.

The church took off with no problem. After a couple of months, people obviously knew something new was in the works because they began coming regularly. It was exciting to watch this grow.

After several months of growth I felt encouraged to go to a minister's conference. Even though we could not afford it, the church thought it a good idea. So with their encouragement we scraped together our few extra dollars and away we went.

During several meetings the Lord kept prompting me to pledge an offering to the special project the conference organizers were telling us about.

Finally I told Dixie what I sensed the Lord saying, and she said she was sensing the same thing. We decided to pray about it during our next meeting and see what God wanted us to do.

During the next meeting, when the offering time came, we both asked the Lord to show us what He wanted us to do.

In my mind I immediately sensed Him say, "$10,000." I just about choked, but I asked Dixie what she received and she had written it down on a scrap of paper.

I told her what I sensed Him saying, knowing she would laugh me out of the building. But instead she showed me her scrap, on which she had penned "10k, which is…"

"Are you kidding me?" I cried. That night we pledged $10,000, adamantly promising the Lord that we would pay it as quickly as He brought it to us.

As we put our pledge in the passing basket it felt scary and exhilarating at the same time. God had to make this come about because we didn't have it – or anything else, as far as that goes.

We were just blessed to be able to attend and hoped we had enough left over for gas to get us back home.

One day, several weeks after our conference, a manila envelope came in the mail containing some official-looking forms and papers concerning a 501k.

When I left the employers I had been working for I cashed in my retirement money to live. A country church of 100 people cannot pay a pastor enough to live, so we had to do something. I always believed that where God guides, God provides.

Up until that point we saw Him guide, but the provision was rather limited.

As I read the information, it seemed that a company I had never worked for, Wells Fargo, was informing me that they had well over $11,000 that belonged to me in a 501k retirement account.

All I had to do was return the sheets signed, include my social security number in the proper spot and they would then cut me a check.

I called their number to check this thing out, and the young lady and her manager reassured me that they had money for me.

I told them I had never worked for their company and they explained that through some company acquisitions, their records showed that I did in fact have some money they needed to disburse to me.

I signed the paper, gave them my social and sent them the paper in the prepaid envelope. Then I waited. A week later the stage coach pulled up to my mail box and deposited a check for well over 11 grand.

That check paid off our $10,000 pledge, a credit card and took us all out to celebrate.

Where God guides, God provides! He is always on time! He never fails! He is all powerful. You can trust Him!

That experience taught me He can be trusted. I have never been concerned about finances, or lack thereof, since that day.

It also freed me from working for money. If we work only for money, we will never be free. God wants us to work for purpose, principle and vision. We are to create more than just the paycheck.

God will never bring anything to us that He can't get through us.

Since that time our ministry has received many individual gifts and offerings that have numbered in the thousands. When we sense God calling us to give, we get excited because we know we shall reap as we give.

He is faithful! Trust Him!

Chapter 13
Holy Boldness For Battle

*I*n 1991, not too long after Holy Spirit and the stage coach blessed us, our new church was holding Wednesday evening bible studies in our home.

We had around 24 in attendance on a normal Wednesday. One of the women who regularly attended had invited two of her coworkers to come one particular Wednesday; two young ladies.

Both of them had been attending for several weeks when I received a visit from one of them during the middle of the week. She was crying at my door when she told me of her need for help.

She said, "My father has been given only six months to live. He is dying from lung cancer and my mother is very sick with lupus and we are not sure how long she has to live. The doctors won't give us a prognosis.

"Will you go to the hospital and visit my father? You'll probably see my mother there. She's there night and day with him."

I asked her if her father or mother knew Jesus, and whether or not they had a church or pastor they, or I, should notify.

She said they never went to church much, unfortunately.

After a few more questions, it seemed like the Lord wanted me to go visit this couple, so I told her I would go see them in the next day or two.

The day came, and I took off for the hospital. As I traveled, I prayed, as I usually did, asking the Lord for the grace to minister according to His will. I wanted Him to make the room clear for private ministry and for the Spirit to build me up spiritually (1 Corinthians 14:4 and Jude 20).

I had no idea what I was going to find, or what their attitude and state of mind would be. I just needed to be prepared for anything, and everything.

I got to the proper hospital floor, still praying in the Spirit. As I got off the elevator, the words from Proverbs 4:20-22 popped into my mind,

"My son, give attention to my words; Incline your ear to my sayings. Do not let them depart from

your eyes, keep them in the midst of your heart; for they are life to those who find them, and health to all their flesh."

I knew the Lord was either going to do something, or He was concerned about me getting sidetracked. I made my way to the proper room, still praying in the Spirit.

As I found the door, I sensed the Spirit of God move within me. As I walked through the door, into the man's room, a miraculous boldness came upon me and I felt like I was walking into the middle of a tremendous fight.

My adrenalin began to flow, my breathing and my heart rate increased and I am sure my nostrils flared in pure defiance for the coming action.

I must have appeared to the people in the room like John the Baptist appeared to those in Judea; a wild man, dressed in camel hair with a leather belt who had been eating bugs and honey. (Matthew 3:3-4.)

My message at that moment was just like John's, "*Repent*, for the Kingdom of Heaven is at hand!"

As I approached the bed I saw a man lying there, obviously very sick, talking to someone in the room, although I paid no attention to the person he was talking to.

It was like everything was blocked out of my view except the man in bed; he alone was the target of my mission.

I remember it was as though I was beside myself, witnessing everything as if I was watching someone else. It definitely was not me – mild-mannered me – springing into action. This is not what I would have normally done.

As soon as he and I locked eyes I began to let him have it by blurting out in a very firm and probably rather loud voice.

"Do you want to live or do you want to die? If you want to live you can! You don't have to die! The devil would like you and your family to believe that the doctors are the only ones who know what is going to happen to you.

"But I'm here to tell you that you can live," and then I paused and, looking him straight in the eye, said, "*If* you turn to Jesus Christ right now!"

For the next two minutes I preached, non-stop, about the man's need for a Savior and how God sent Jesus to earth to become our sacrifice so we could have God living in us.

I ended it with, "Now if you've got God in you, you've got all that God *is*, living in you!

"Is God sick? Is God broke? Is God confused? Of *course* He isn't! So tell me, do you want to live or do you want to die?"

The guy's eyes were bugged out; I thought they were going to pop out of his head. His mouth was open so far I think his chin rested on his chest.

Then I shouted one last question, "Do you want to live or do you want to die? Time for you to decide!"

I had my eyes focused on his and it was like I was made of steel. I couldn't move! I could only stare into his eyes. I think for that moment I actually scared the hell right out of that man and out of the entire room to boot.

He started shaking his head yes and he stammered, "I... want to... live." So immediately, out of my mouth came, "Then you've got to ask Jesus Christ into your heart right now!"

I took his hands and led him in a quick prayer of surrender to Christ Jesus. The power of God was so strong in that room I could hardly stand.

Up until that very moment, I had not even given any thought to others who may have been in the room. But as I prayed with him, the Spirit of God told me to do the same thing to the woman behind me.

Immediately upon finishing our fervent prayer, I wheeled around like a ninja warrior defending himself from an attacker and I let her have it with both spiritual barrels.

I remember thinking to myself about this time, "What in the world is going on? This is powerful!"

I had confidence in exactly what was going to happen, and things were moving so fast I could only hang on to my confidence in what God was doing and go along for the ride.

And what a ride it was!

I said exactly the same thing to the woman and preached the exact message to her that I had just preached to the man. I remember adding only one thing different when I began.

"And the same thing goes for you, too, Lady!" Then I began by telling her she didn't have to die, that she could live.

As I ministered to the lady, I remember noticing her complexion. She was almost yellow; a garish, pasty yellow and her eyes looked funny, almost deranged. I had never seen anything like that before and I never have since.

At the end, I led her in the same prayer as the one I did the man in bed. After the prayer, I did an about-face and left the room immediately.

Usually when ministering to the sick, I would have hung around a little bit to exchange some pleasantries. Not this time. For some strange reason I felt an urgency to leave. So I did.

Once I got on the elevator I began to notice my breathing rate. It was like I had just run a marathon. My heart was pounding and when the elevator began to move I almost felt sick.

This was the first time I actually felt like I was possessed by God. It was exhilarating, but at the same time I was very glad I was out of that room. I hoped they wouldn't call security and have me arrested at the front door.

Thank God they didn't and I wasn't.

Whew! I was home free.

***

Several weeks later, I had managed to put that whole experience out of my mind, when all of a sudden, the young lady who asked me to visit with her father and mother showed up at the door.

She was all excited and I thought, for a moment, that she might want to kill me for what I had done to her parents.

She came in and reported, "My dad said you were there and the very next day the doctors ran some final tests on his lungs and released him from the hospital.

"The bottom line is, they told him something must have gone wrong because he had no sign of cancer in him! They sent him home.

"What did you say to my mom? She has never been the same since you talked to her in Dad's room. Her complexion has changed and she says she has never felt so good in her life. I think she is healed too."

And on and on she went, so fast I had to slow her down occasionally to make sure I was hearing her properly.

Both of these people were healed and haven't suffered from these diseases since.

I'll never forget the Spirit of God and His boldness that came upon me that day.

I have only had that type of supernatural boldness come upon me one other time, and that resulted in an elderly couple with very hard and indifferent hearts toward God confessing Jesus as their Lord and receiving Him as their Savior.

There have been several times when I wish I could be that bold, but in my natural demeanor I could never work up that type of raw power.

God knew the type of spiritual enemy I would be facing that day and, basically, no devil can operate when Holy Spirit powers the Body of Christ to take authority.

The only way Holy Spirit can empower anyone is for us to give Him permission by our total surrender to Him.

Only then will the spiritual work be accomplished as it should be, so we can respond and follow God, and become holy vessels of honor that He can then anoint.

Remember, in Luke 10:19 Jesus said,

"Behold, I give you the authority to trample on serpents and scorpions, and over all the power of the enemy, and nothing shall by any means hurt you."

The Lord powered me to walk in that authority that day, and we resoundingly trampled the enemy.

Two people came to Jesus, both were healed from life threatening diseases, the hospital and attending doctors saw a miracle, the couple's daughter witnessed the supernatural power of God and the enemy was defeated and run out the door.

Chapter 14
If God Is For Us

"What then shall we say to these things? If God is for us, who can be against us? He who did not spare His own Son, but delivered Him up for us all, how shall He not with Him also freely give us all things?"
(Romans 8:31, 32)

The telephone was ringing off the hook, both in my dream and in the kitchen.

The sun was just beginning to chase away the darkness of the early morning as I stumbled my way to the phone, still half asleep.

Clearing my throat so I sounded half-way coherent and with some level of control, I answered and was met by a frantic plea for help from an apparently young woman.

The caller rushed into her plea for help without even so much as a hello, or a good morning. She was frantic, and in a rush to receive my answer and get on with the task at hand, whatever my answer would be.

"Pastor, I desperately need you to help me! They are going to unplug my cousin this morning and I need you to help me with the family. Most of them don't know God and I know it's going to be a terrible mess. Would you please help me? *Please!*"

My head was still spinning from the quick trip to the phone. Concentrating, I said, "Hold on, hold on! What do you mean they are going to unplug your cousin?"

She apologized for being so abrupt and for it being so early in the morning. She said, "I just don't know who else to turn to."

She began to tell me about the situations in her cousin's life that put him in the hospital, nearly dead.

She told me her 34 year-old cousin, Dennis, had been in trouble since he was six years old. She told me the abbreviated story of his life; how he had served quite a bit of time for dealing drugs and had just recently gotten released from the state penitentiary.

She explained how he had returned home to a very hostile family situation and the wrong friends, and in desperate need for money; and how, four days before he had tried, a second time, to end his life by overdosing on his prescription medication.

The overdose actually killed him and the emergency medics responding to the 911 call from his wife got his heart restarted and took him to the emergency ward at Mercy Hospital.

The ER staff and all the attending physicians warned the family that he would probably never live – because of the length of time his brain was without oxygen and the strength of the drugs that, by this time, were circulated throughout his system.

They gave him very little hope of ever again being anything but a vegetable, even if his body would support itself after the life support system was removed.

State law permitted that after 18 to 24 hours of no traceable brain waves or activity, the hospital could, upon the request of the family, unplug the life support and let the body quit operating on its own.

This was Dennis' morning to be "unplugged," because he had been hooked up to life support without any brain activity for over 38 hours.

The family finally agreed to allow the hospital to prepare him and unplug him. Therefore, the entire family had been called in to see Dennis one last time before they released him from his tragic life.

The sun was now lighting up the house and I knew my day had started. What a start!

"Would you please go with me to the hospital?" she asked. "I don't want to face all those people without some prayer help."

She went on to tell that there might even be some serious trouble with some of Dennis' "friends," who promised to raise hell, and she wanted to spare Dennis' parents anymore pain from his sordid life of drugs and crime.

I don't know what she thought I could do against a crew of brainless thugs that thought it macho to cause a grieving family trouble on a day like this.

I said, "Yes, I'll go with you, but first I have to take a shower."

"Great!" she cried "I'll pick you up in a few minutes, but we have to hurry because they are going to unplug him by 9 o'clock this morning."

Immediately my mind went to work, acting cowardly. "Man! I can't believe what I get myself into! *When* will I ever learn to say no?"

During my shower I started having a not-so-nice conversation with God.

"When are you going to bring me live people, God? When are you going to have people come to me that have no problems? Why don't you bring normal people to me like you do other pastors?

"Why can't you bring these people to me before the devil kills them, God?"

And on and on I grumbled, until I had finished getting ready and was getting into the car to leave for the hospital with Laura, my anxious young caller.

During the first few minutes of the trip to the hospital I repented, while Laura tried to tell me more about Dennis' life.

I already knew more than I wanted to, and I just needed some quiet, so I said, "Laura, do you mind if we just pray the rest of the way to the hospital? I really need to hear from God."

For the rest of the hour trip I stared out the side window and prayed in the Spirit, hoping I hadn't grumbled my way into problems with God.

I am so thankful that we serve a God of grace and mercy. I thank God He is a forgiving Father who understands the weakness of our flesh and knows our heart so thoroughly.

When we arrived at the hospital, my heart was pounding as I told my mind to hush. I could just see us getting into some sort of a drug dealers' battle over this young man's body or something.

We made our way to the family's waiting room on the intensive care floor; all the while I was praying in the Spirit – more to keep my mind off the situation than to prepare myself to minister.

We entered the room where every seat was taken. Everyone there was waiting for the nurses to prepare Dennis' body so the family could go see him before unplugging his life-support system.

Laura very politely introduced me to everyone in the room as her pastor. She explained that I had consented to minister to their needs during this terrible, life-altering experience.

The family and friends of Dennis didn't seem impressed, nor should they have, with the heavy burden of Dennis' life, struggles and his apparently successful suicide weighing them down.

Laura and I took the last two seats on a four-person couch and waited, and waited and waited. All the time I was praying in the Spirit, pleading with God to do jump right in so I could do something besides just wait and watch this family suffer in silence.

Suddenly, a woman sitting across the room began to weep openly and wailed, "He can't die! I prayed all night that he wouldn't die! He just can't!"

The events of the next few minutes following that outburst changed my life and ministry forever. They took me on an adventure wherein God was able to teach me wonderful things about instant obedience to the voice of God, faith and the power of the Holy Spirit within us and upon us.

"That's why he *won't* die." I said.

Suddenly, every eye in that room turned to look at me, and it became deathly still as the woman I was answering said, "What did you say?" as she stared at me in shock.

An entire book could be written about the heavy thoughts that were going through my mind at that very moment.

I couldn't believe I had said that. "Where did that come from?" I thought to myself as the room waited for my reply.

I said, rather sheepishly, "If he doesn't die it's because you prayed all night."

And everybody went back to their waiting, while inside I breathed a sigh of relief that no one wanted to question me about the comment I just made.

"Thank God I got out of that one!" I thought.

I knew what I had said, and it played over and over in my mind so loudly that I was sure everyone could hear it, "What do you mean, 'He won't die,' Lord?" I questioned. "I thought he was already dead!"

At that very moment the words, "Lead her to Me. She doesn't know who I am!" came into my mind. I knew it was God and He was about to do something!

I turned to Laura and asked her, "Who is that woman who is crying?"

She told me it was Dennis' mother.

After asking Laura if his mother or father were Christians and finding out that neither was, I asked Laura to invite them to talk with me while I asked a nurse if there was a private room to meet in.

The nurse took us to a little conference room just across the hall from Dennis' intensive care room.

I shared the Gospel with them and explained to the best of my ability how we need Jesus. After a few minutes I asked them if they could believe in – and receive – Jesus as their personal Savior.

They looked at each other and said, "Yes. We sure do need something."

As I prayed with them to receive Jesus, the Lord inserted into my mind the following instructions.

"As you leave this room, the nurses will be ready to call the family. Before anyone else comes down, take his mother, father, Laura and two other Christian family members in and pray around Dennis' bed.

"Place his mother up by his head and have the rest of them encircle the bed. Have his mother tell him that she just received Jesus as her personal Savior and that she loves Him."

At that moment we said "amen," and I asked them if they knew what they had just done. We talked a little bit about their salvation and just what that meant to them for the near and distant future.

I then asked them if there were any other family members that were Christians here besides Laura.

They told me that both Dennis' sister and aunt were both Christian and they were in the waiting room.

I had Laura go get the two Christian ladies just like the Lord told me, while the rest of us stepped out the door of the conference room into the hall of the intensive care unit.

Just then, the door to Dennis' room swung open and the first nurse that came out said, "He is ready for you now, whenever you are," as the team of other nurses disappeared down the hall.

Laura came down the hall with the two ladies that I vaguely remembered meeting when we first arrived. We all stepped into Dennis' room and I shut the door behind us. He was bloated and swollen and his complexion was an ash gray color.

Well, it looked like Dennis had finally succeeded in leaving this world. We all stood there and looked at this poor mass of flesh that had suffered so in life.

Dennis had a round scar on the right side of his head where he had suffered a gunshot wound years before. He had two thick scars like a necklace running around his throat from ear to ear where someone had cut his throat in an attempt to kill him.

His wrists were scarred where he had tried ending his own life. He had burn marks on his body from who knows what.

It was obvious that his life had been an absolute, pathetic mess.

"What a terrible life of pain," I thought, while the family was crying and saying, "We're sorry Dennis. We failed you. We love you, and we hope you are not in pain anymore."

I asked them to all take their positions around the bed as the Lord had instructed me. Then we joined hands and I told his mother to tell him she was a new Christian.

"Why?" she wailed. "He's dead now! He can't hear me!"

Out of my mouth came, "He will hear you. Just tell him and then we will pray."

Reluctantly and tearfully his mother bent over to his ear and told him of her new found faith and then she kissed him on the cheek and said, "Goodbye, son. I am very sorry. I love you very much."

"Let's pray!" I cried, and I knew exactly what the Lord wanted me to say; very simple, short, and sweet.

I said, "Death angel, I bind you and release you from duty against this young man and I call life back into Dennis' body in Jesus' Name!"

Immediately his eyes opened, his body began to jerk and he sat straight up!

Startled and fearful, we all jumped back!

The door flew open and nurses came scrambling from everywhere, madly ordering us to leave the room!

I was most happy to oblige them.

Mom, dad, aunts, cousin and I all returned to the waiting room where everyone else was oblivious to what had just taken place.

Our experience didn't remain a secret for long as the family began to dance around, excitedly sharing what had just taken place.

I found a quiet corner to retreat to and pray. I, too, was rather confounded about what had just happened. After all, I had merely repeated what I believe God had told me to say, which was all I could've done.

As I contemplated what had just taken place, a doctor appeared at the door to make an announcement. Total silence fell over the room as he said, "I have some good news and some not so good news.

"The good news is Dennis' body is currently operating on its own.

"The bad news is Dennis' brain has been dormant for far too long to expect anything good to come out of this. I am sorry, but Dennis will more than likely end up either being a vegetable or a raving mad man for as long as he lives.

"Right now, he is a raving mad man and he must be securely restrained."

At that moment I found myself leaping to my feet and shouting emphatically, "What God began, God will complete!" Then I sat back down sheepishly.

The doctor said, "Excuse me?" It was as though he couldn't believe what he had just heard. His look said, "Who are *you* to contradict what I just said?"

I then found myself saying, "If God raised him from the dead, He will make him whole again."

The doctor turned on his heals to leave as he said, "Well, we will see about that! But for now, don't expect much from Dennis!"

Everything went crazy for about a half an hour. His roughneck friends were spouting things like, "Unbelievable! I don't get it; the SOB just won't die!"

I was more concerned about a fight breaking out than anything. I prayed frantically for God's peace to come and restore calm to this atmosphere of chaos, fear and uncertainty.

Nobody knew for sure what happened. Doctors and nurses were saying that he was never going to know anything or anybody. His brain had been dead too long.

This just couldn't be happening!

But it *was* happening; and the Christian family members and I were praying in the Spirit like crazy as the rest of the family sat there dumb-founded!

Dennis had returned from the dead!

He was alive and eventually called for his wife and other members of his family. The only problem was, he was very angry, uncontrollable and wanted to kill everyone. So they kept him restrained as he ranted and raved until his voice finally gave out.

I knew the work wasn't done yet, but things certainly became exciting all of a sudden. The Lord directed me to gather his Christian relatives and pray for two main things in Dennis' life.

First was to bind the spirit of suicide from his life and loose him from operating against him. Second was to pray that Dennis would gain a desire to live and call for help.

I also knew that we were not to go see him until he called out for help, no matter how long it took.

As I explained this information to his sister, aunt and Laura, his sister protested about not going to see him. I told her I didn't understand the details but I was convinced it was from God and we'd better obey it if we wanted Dennis to be free.

That night we all met for prayer at his sister's house and prayed exactly what the Lord God had told us to pray.

During our time of prayer a great peace settled upon us and we instinctively knew something was finished; our job was over, victory was at hand.

We all looked at each other and agreed. Something significant had just happened and we could call it a night.

As we all went our separate ways, we promised each other we would keep praying for Dennis until we heard from him. I made his sister promise me that she would call the moment she heard anything.

Several days went by and I heard nothing. I was beginning to think I'd had a very long and detailed dream. So I called Dennis' sister to see if it had really happened and if she heard anything from Dennis or his condition.

She said it really did happen and that they had finally released Dennis from the ICU and transferred him to a mental hospital just a few miles away.

At this point, the doctors were saying that there seemed to be nothing physically wrong with him at all. However, he was still exceedingly angry and uncontrollable, so he was restrained by a straight jacket in his private, well-padded room.

Several days went by, until one morning I received a phone call from Dennis' sister.

"You are not going to believe this!" she enthused. "Dennis just called me and told me that he wanted to live and would I please send someone up to help him.

"Would you please go Pastor?" she asked.

I was excited to go – and a little apprehensive at the same time. I had never been in a mental ward where people had to be restrained and locked up.

I had ministered a couple of times in mental institutions before, but they were all minimum security facilities and I never sensed any danger, only compassion for the hurting people who were there.

I left immediately, praying and praising God all the way to the hospital.

Parking my car in the clergy parking stall, I reminded the Lord that He had begun this work on Dennis and I was depending upon Him to carry it out to completion (Philippians 1:6) because I had no idea what to do next.

As a matter of fact, I told the Lord that I was shaking in my boots. As if I had to tell *Him*. I asked Him to remove my fear (1 John 4:18) so I could at least appear to be composed and in control.

After ringing the buzzers and talking to a voice over a speaker, the door buzzed and a voice said, "You may enter now, but wait for the inside door to be opened by the orderly."

The orderly finally came after what seemed an eternity and welcomed me in.

After signing in and proving my identity with ID, he escorted me to Dennis' room.

As we walked down the long corridor lined with heavy locked doors, the orderly told me to only *talk* to him and do not, under *any* circumstances, touch him or offer to help him do anything. I was not to pass him anything or promise him anything.

He told me that I would be on camera and that I should call out for help if I needed anything or felt at all uneasy or unsafe.

"Any questions?" he asked.

As I replied, "I don't think so," he opened the door to a very unsettling room about eight feet square with heavy army green padding on the walls and floor. The light bulb was at least 12 feet above us and covered in steel mesh. There was one cot-like bed but no bedding like I was accustomed too.

On the cot sat a man, cross legged and wrapped securely in a straight-jacket, swaying quietly, staring straight ahead at the chair that had been set for me.

As the orderly shut the door behind me he said, "Remember, call if you need any help or become uneasy!"

I didn't say anything, but I was aware that I was already uneasy.

In a quick glance around the room, trying not to act fearful or suspicious, I noticed the camera high in the corner reminding me that Dennis and I were being watched and every move was being recorded.

The whole scene was quite daunting and overwhelming for someone's first visit. Yes, I was nervous, to say the least. To be honest, I was terrified.

So, there I was in Dennis' room and there he was, the man raised from the dead only a week before. He just stared at me and said not a single word.

I had never seen a strait jacket before and I found myself staring at him like a kid at a circus freak show.

He couldn't do anything without help.

The extra-long sleeves were wrapped around him, crossing his arms over his chest and stretched to the back, where a piece from his mid-section that went under his crotch and up the back, all met and were securely locked together.

I really mean locked – like with a key-type lock where only an orderly with a key could free him. I had never seen such a thing except in a movie once, but this was very real, very eye-opening and very sobering.

The first words we finally exchanged were absolutely wonderful.

"That looks terribly uncomfortable," I said. Dennis just looked at me with a slight, wry smile and said in a very gravelly voice, "I've been worse."

I introduced myself and he said, "I know. My sister said you would come."

I asked him what I could do for him and he began to tell me about his pitiful life, how many times he had tried to kill himself and how many times he had been in jail because he kept trying to kill himself.

He told me how many times he had been shot and beat up, in prison and out. He told me he could not remember wanting to live. I could feel the pain in his voice.

He told me when, at six years old, he set fire to his family's trailer home. He also told me of times as a child getting beaten with boards and bats, and of eating poison in a sandwich, trying to kill himself when he was a teenager because he hurt so much.

He finally said, "Something came over me this morning. I don't know how to explain it, except it's like I just woke up from a very long nightmare and I knew I wanted to live and do something with my life.

"I can't believe I'm saying this, but I really do want to live. I've seen death too many times and evidently God doesn't want me to die yet. That definitely means something.

"So I need help to learn how to live."

I explained that Jesus was the Life of men and women and that He came and died as a sacrifice for our sinful selves. I told Dennis that every sin that human beings have ever committed, no matter how heinous, have all been forgiven and all we must do is understand that Jesus paid our debt and receive Him and what He did by faith. Then we would be saved.

Dennis did believe that day. He bowed his head with me and I led him in prayer to confess Jesus as his personal Lord and Savior.

As soon as we pronounced, "Amen," Dennis began to speak in other tongues.

He was so excited he began to bounce up and down on his bed until he fell right off, on his head, still speaking in tongues, laughing and crying, making me wonder if he was okay.

I wanted to help him but I remember the stern instructions the orderly gave me about not helping him for *any* reason!

Just then an orderly came in to help Dennis back onto his bed. It was quite an unfathomable scene to behold.

The orderly, a big burly fellow, picked up Dennis and placed him back onto his bed asking, "What in the world is going on in here?"

Before I could say anything, Dennis said, "I just found life! I'm going to live! Jesus just forgave me and I'm going to live."

The orderly said, "Well, if you keep falling on your head like that, Jesus is going to have to do more than just save your soul, brother. He's gonna have to give you a new head!" At that he laughed as he left us together to pray with each other.

The day after he accepted Jesus, the hospital staff realized something powerful had happened to Dennis because of his outward glow and new behavior.

Because of that they allowed him to put on his own clothes and eventually assigned him to a room with a window, some bedding and regular walls and floors.

Dennis stayed in the mental hospital for several weeks after his conversion and I visited him as often as I could. We had bible studies together and we prayed as he planned on what he was going to do when he got out.

Dennis had many ups and downs after that. It was hard keeping up with him. He had more time to serve because of some drug deals and other crimes he was caught up in before he decided to end it all.

My wife and I visited him several times and wrote to him all the time he was in jail.

The rest of the story? Tragically, he drank bleach. We tried to help him find inner peace but he wouldn't go there.

Dennis lived several more years, got married, had another son and died of liver disease 10 years later.

I have run into his wife and son a couple of times since. They are a constant reminder of Dennis' miracle. His son is a product of that miracle.

There is truly *nothing* that will separate us from the love of God that is in Christ Jesus. This God of ours reaches down into hell itself and brings up those who are being prayed for. Jesus wants no one to perish without the opportunity to know Him. (Romans 8:38, 39)

Chapter 15
One More Year

The days of our lives are seventy years; and if by reason of strength they are eighty years, yet their boast is only labor and sorrow; For it is soon cut off, and we fly away." (Psalm 90:10)

*I*n December of 1992 we were in the middle of our kids' Christmas program, when Bob, a man who had only recently been coming to our church, approached me anxiously.

"I've just received a message that my mother is dying and all the family has been called in," he related. "Will you come to the hospital with me?"

I was filling in on the sound board that year and we were right in the middle of our program. The Spirit of God was moving; and between God and our little children everyone was being blessed wonderfully.

There were tables of goodies to be shared at the end of our program and I was definitely looking forward to meeting some of the people who had come as visitors. I wanted to make their acquaintance and encourage them to make our church their home. However, God had other plans for me that evening.

I told Bob that I had to finish the program on the sound, but as soon as the program was over and the socializing had begun, I would come straight away to the hospital.

The final curtain call was given, all the little children filed out on stage in costume with their Sunday school teachers and all the helpers who had worked so hard making the Christmas program the best ever.

The announcement was given for all the visitors to stay for fellowship and to share in all the goodies that our women had provided. The lights came on in the auditorium and the '92 Christmas program was over, soon to become a fond memory.

I was having a terrible time leaving that auditorium. But I knew the importance of my being at the hospital to minister to this anxious family who was about to lose their mother and grandmother.

"What a terrible, inopportune time to lose a loved one!" I thought.

I finally found my coat, told my wife where I was going and asked a few of the men to make sure things were cleaned up and put away. Out the door I went.

I really thought that I would run to the hospital, pray for Bob's mother, pray with the family, offer them a few words of comfort, and be able to return to the Christmas celebration, being hardly missed.

However, that is certainly not what God had in mind for me this fateful evening.

On the way to the hospital, I prayed in the Spirit in order to partly prepare myself to minister and to mostly forget the wonderful social time I was missing.

It was late, around 9 p.m., so it wasn't hard to find a convenient parking space. I got to the cardiac ICU floor and headed toward the family waiting area.

Bob noticed me the same moment I spotted him. He came running to me and said, "I'm glad you made it. Mom is not doing very well and the doctors say she will be gone by morning. Shall we go pray for her?"

As I saw the concern in Bob's eyes I felt guilty for thinking about my own petty inconveniences.

My hopes of a quick return suddenly died as I realized that this was not going to be a quick hand-patting tour.

Under my breath I began to repent, asking God to forgive me for such insensitivity – again, because I didn't know how to pray effectively I also allowed the Holy Spirit to quietly pray through me.

Peace and comfort always comes just knowing the Holy Spirit is with me when I have no clue what to do next – which, to be honest, is most of the time.

Before going to pray for his mother, I first asked him to introduce me to the rest of the family. I needed some time and information to get prepared for the unknown that lay before us.

I had been in CICU units before and they are never pleasant. That's why it is called *intensive* care; serious life and death decisions are made every minute in the CICU.

It's never easy to watch someone die; plus I wanted to know something more about those who I would be ministering too while we waited for the doctors' predictions to come to pass.

From the beginning of this adventure I assumed she was a very old woman and her body must simply be worn out.

After a few minutes of light talk and the first introductions, Bob said, "Shouldn't we go pray for her now?" So Bob, his wife, children and I went to go pray for Grandma.

On the way to the CICU I asked God what He wanted me to do and how He wanted me to pray. I surrendered to Him so He could speak through me.

I recognized that this family was looking to me to help them! And at that moment God spoke to me and said, "That's the trouble!"

As that Word came, I knew immediately what God meant and that He was going to help them trust *Him*. Another thought that was strong in my mind was that I had to be ready to seize the opportunities to point them to their real source of help – Jesus.

Grandma was definitely in bad shape. The doctors had said that her heart wasn't working as it should and she had therefore retained a lot of water causing swelling in her face. Worst of all, water was filling the cavity around her heart and her lungs.

They kept emphasizing the fact that she only had a few hours at the most to live.

"So make sure your family is notified," they said.

Her face was swollen, and the oxygen tube carrying oxygen to her lungs through her nose was buried in her swollen flesh. She was laboring terribly for air. It was definitely close to the end for her.

I asked the family to join hands with me and we all prayed silently for a little while as their Grandma struggled to breathe, fighting for life.

I couldn't seem to get anything definite from God, so I just prayed that the doctors and nurses would receive wisdom and knowledge from Heaven.

I also asked God to put His hand on this woman and make her journey easier and for her family. I ended with asking Him to give me wisdom to minister by His Spirit, in Jesus' Name.

That prayer seemed so little and so powerless; I felt terrible and I know the family was probably thinking. "I could have done that! Where's the power this man always preaches about?"

Although they never said it, I could feel it. We returned to the waiting room to wait.

The hardest job in the world is to wait, especially when you are waiting for God to do something or for someone to die. It is not in us, human beings, to wait.

But we did, because we were so helpless in this situation and definitely needed God.

We just sat and waited; killing time by watching TV, playing cards or just wondering how to not think of the things that bothered us so, like someone dying.

Or if one is really desperate, they wait while praying in their spirit language. And that is what I was doing – praying in my spirit language, quietly and to myself, desperately hoping God would do something to relieve the tension in this situation.

It seemed as if hours had ticked by as I watched that family try so hard to act normally, fighting back tears and against painful memories, arguing with each other over trivial matters, all in an attempt to *not* think of what was happening just down the hall.

Actually, only about 30 minutes went by from the time we were in the CICU until I sensed the Lord saying to me, "My Word promises humankind three score and 10!"

At that moment I knew instinctively that God was trying to help me. I said, "Bob, how old is your mother?"

"She would have been 69 next month," he replied.

I kept thinking about the Word that came to me and about their grandma's age. "She's only 69, Lord," I prayed. "You promised us 70 years according to Your Scriptures (Psalm 90:10). What are You trying to tell me, Lord?"

I kept thinking and praying silently in the Spirit about this for about another half hour without saying anything to anybody.

Suddenly, I sensed in my mind these words, "Tell them I'll give her one more year for the purpose of getting to know Me and for patching up family relationships."

I knew God had spoken. It was unmistakable to me. But I didn't want to tell them what I had just received. After all, I had made plenty of mistakes before and this was one mistake that I did not want to make.

So I just sat there and in my mind prayed, "Father if this is from You, You tell them and have them ask me and I'll confirm it."

This seemed like a fair deal to me, so I kept waiting and praying in the Spirit while the Word kept going around and around in my head.

Finally, a Word came to me that said, "Tell them!"

"But God!" I thought. "This is so hard! Why can't *You* tell them?"

And I heard again, "*Tell them!*" This time I knew God wasn't going to make a deal with me and I knew I had to tell them what I sensed God telling me.

"God has promised us 70 years," I said. Everyone focused their attention on me and Bob's wife told the kids to turn down the TV. Then she said, "What did you say?"

"God has promised us 70 years. Your mother is still too young to die," I said again.

And then I followed that up with, "Bob, would you and your wife come out in the hall with me? I have something I must tell you."

I got up and walked out to the hall, followed by Bob, his wife, his daughter and sons.

We should have just stayed in the waiting room, but I desperately wanted some privacy. For what I was about to tell them, I didn't want to take any chances of being overheard by others in the room.

When I had them alone I said, "I believe God has spoken to my heart about your mother. I believe God said He'll give her one more year to get to know Him and to patch up her relationships with you."

As soon as I said that, Bob's wife and daughter began to violently weep.

I thought they were just excited about what I had just shared, and they were. But I learned later that there had been some terrible feelings between Bob's wife and his mother.

There had been a genuine feud going on for as long as anyone could remember between this woman and others in her family. There was true hatred toward one another and many mixed emotions ran wild through these folks as I relayed this message to them.

Bob was beginning to get very excited and joyful. He recognized this was definitely a Word from the Lord because there was no way I could have known about the family problems.

He kept saying, "She's going to be all right! She's going to be all right! She's going to be all right!"

Just then a nurse rounded the corner and Bob ran over to her and said, "Pastor Larry said Mom's going to be all right! God told Him! Will it be all right if we go home now and come back in the morning?"

I wanted to crawl into a hole as the nurse looked disgustedly at me and then directly in Bob's eyes.

"No, you can't go home!" she hissed. "Your mother is dying and probably has only an hour or two left!" Then she wheeled around and stormed angrily down the hall back to the CICU.

As Bob looked at me with the question of, "*Now* who do I believe?" in his eyes, I said, "Bob, let's let God be God and just wait a little while longer and see how He's going to do it."

At that we went back to the waiting room. Several hours went by and we made several trips in and out of the CICU to pray for Grandma and to comfort relatives who arrived throughout the night.

With every person who came into the waiting room, excitable Bob said, "Don't worry. Pastor heard from God and Mom's going to live at least one more year!" And as he told them they turned to see what kind of a nut would say something like that.

I began to hate seeing all the people entering that room!

We kept waiting until on one of our trips to the care unit, the nurse on duty said, "There has been a slight improvement in your mother's condition. It's still touch and go, but things have improved quite a bit. You can all go home if you would like and we will call you if there is a turn for the worse."

Praise the Lord! The words I had been waiting for had arrived! Now I could get out of there and have a talk with God that I knew He would hear. But on my way to the car I had a strange, peaceful feeling that everything was going to be all right.

At least three times a week I would go to that CICU room in hopes of finding that woman totally healed. Every time I left thinking, "Well, at least she is still alive. She has a chance to make amends. Praise You, Jesus!"

I did that four weeks in a row and things didn't seem to be getting any better for her – until one day during the fourth week I walked up to the room and there she was, sitting up in bed, eating.

I walked in and said, "How are you, young lady?" She said, "Fine, Doctor. I suppose you're here to get some more blood."

I introduced myself to her and reassured her I wasn't there for blood.

For the next 11 months I was able to minister to her, helping her understand her need for a Savior and praying with her to receive Jesus into her life.

We also worked together on getting those family relationships patched up and I witnessed a great healing between her and her family as she learned how to forgive and to receive forgiveness.

Exactly 11 months from the day she got out of the hospital, Grandma went home to be with Jesus.

Just a few days short of one full year from the night I sat in the waiting room and heard

God say He'd give her one more year to take care of business.

During Grandma's last year, I was never able to minister to her husband. He would never come to church he wouldn't allow me to minister to him at his home.

I talked to him in the hospital and he was grateful for his wife's healing. He thanked me every time he saw me. I kept telling him that I didn't heal her, God did, but he would never allow me to talk to him about the Lord.

Two days after his wife passed away, Bob and I were ministering to him, when Grandpa said, "I've decided I want to know the same Jesus that Mom knew."

We were so excited! We prayed with him to receive Jesus as his personal Savior right then. We laughed and cried together and had a good time talking about what Heaven was going to be like and how Grandma must be having a great time there.

Bob's dad kept saying, "I want to be where she is! I've got no reason to go on living. We've been together so long I don't know how to live without her."

We kept encouraging him and Bob kept telling him that he had many reasons to live. He had his grandchildren and his family. But Grandpa just kept saying, "I want to be with her, where she is!"

It was getting very late and we finally got Grandpa settled down and into bed.

Bob and I went our separate ways. I went home to prepare for the funeral which was going to be held the next day, while Bob went home to his family to also prepare himself and them for the coming day.

Very early the next morning the phone rang. It was Bob.

"Pastor, Dad's dead." he said.

I couldn't believe what I was hearing. I said, "Speak up, Bob! What did you say?"

"Dad's dead," he said again. "Thank God he asked Jesus into his heart because he went home to be with Jesus last night."

Two days later we had a double funeral, ending the miracle of "one more year" and one of the greatest lessons about listening and following the voice of God I had ever learned to that point.

> *"For as many as are led by the Spirit of God, these are the sons of God."*
> (Romans 8:14 NKJV)

Another great lesson I learned through this experience was how powerful our words and desires are.

Bob's dad desired to be with his wife so much that the words of his mouth translated into action.

Be careful what you ask for.

"For assuredly, I say to you, Whoever says to this mountain, 'Be removed and be cast into the sea,' And does not doubt in his heart, But believes that those things he says will be done, he will have whatever he says." (Mark 11:23)

Chapter 16
The Mask Lady

Several years went by as we worked to construct our new church building. New people were coming and everything was going exceptionally well.

One morning, as I was spending time with the Lord, I received a phone call from a woman I had never met, but had heard about.

The town called her the Mask Lady because she always wore a surgical mask over her face when she was out in public.

She started out our conversation by saying, "People in town say you can help me."

I responded, "I'll try! How can I help?"

"I really need some money so I can go to Denver," she said.

In my mind I was thinking that people don't give a hoot about the church until they need some money.

"Do you have a pastor or a church?" I asked, as I always do.

"No," she said flatly. "I don't know of any church that would take me. In fact, it was the local ministerial association that told me you could help."

Immediately my heart broke for her and I inwardly asked God to forgive my attitude.

"Why are you going to Denver?" I asked.

"To get a lung transplant," was her reply.

It made me angry to think that a ministers association wouldn't be willing to help someone who obviously was in dire straits. I asked her to explain what was going on in her life.

She said, "You've probably seen me around town; I'm the Mask Lady. I'm always on oxygen and I am so weak that I can't go on this way and the medication I am taking just to breathe is deteriorating my bones.

"So, my doctor set me up with an appointment in Denver some time ago to have a lung transplant and they notified me they are ready for me next Monday.

"I just don't have money for the plane ticket or a motel so I can stay in the area while I recuperate."

At that moment the Lord impressed me to invite her to church on Sunday and to give her the money she needed.

I said, "I think the Lord would allow us to help you. But I need you to come to church

Sunday morning so we can make sure you get what you need."

She agreed to come.

Immediately I began to feel the Lord was going to do something, so I prayed that I would be sensitive to the Holy Spirit's leading and that God's will would be done for the ailing Mask Lady.

Sunday morning came and the service was starting with no sign of the Mask Lady.

I alerted the ushers that she might come and to help make sure she was comfortable.

The praise and worship team assembled and began to lead us in worship and there was still no sign of her.

I finally resigned myself that she had chickened out or was too sick or weak and was not coming.

My next thought was what I should do with the check, because I knew God told me to help her financially and invite her to church.

About half way through our praise and worship time, I felt a tap on my shoulder and it was my head usher, telling me, "She's here."

I turned around to see her coming in the sanctuary door and finding her seat. I was surprised and amazed at how young she was. I assumed I was dealing with an older lady but she appeared to be in her 30s or early 40s at the very most.

I said, "What do you want me to do, Lord?" I sensed nothing, so I went back to worshipping, knowing I would meet her after the service.

We had a glorious service that morning; one that you hope would just keep going on and on. Suddenly the Lord said, "Go lay hands on her."

I left my place and headed toward her when she began backing up with fear in her eyes. I tried to reach her to encourage her and pray for her, but she backed into the wall before I could get to her.

She left her oxygen tank at her seat so I wanted to pray for her quickly and get her back to her seat before she passed out from oxygen deprivation.

As I reached out to comfort her she passed out and slid down the wall, ending up sitting on the floor.

I sensed God saying two words, "new lungs." So I laid hands on her shoulder and said, "New lungs in Jesus' Name."

I also sensed the Lord saying, "Leave her right there." So I told the ushers to not touch her and to leave her alone until she asked for or indicated she needed some help.

As I think about it now, it never entered my mind then that we had a woman with bad lungs, off her oxygen, sitting in the corner of the sanctuary obviously unconscious – and we assumed she was breathing!

I remember clearly that I just knew God was doing something huge. I just didn't know how incredibly huge.

When worship ended I went up to the platform, dismissed our children for children's church and preached the message.

The woman never moved until the end of the message, when I noticed her stirring and the ushers helping her to her seat.

After the message I gave an alter call as usual, prayed for a few people and dismissed the service after inviting all to return for the evening service.

My wife and I then made our way down the aisle to invite her into my office where we could talk and offer comfort and support.

We discussed the amount of money she needed and what it was going to do for her. She talked about her children, her husband and why they didn't have the necessary funds. She promised to pay the money back even though I assured her it was not necessary.

She told me what time her plane left in the morning and who was going to take her to the airport. But never once did she mention sliding down the wall and sitting unconscious for the majority of the service.

I told her we would help her in any way we could. I asked her to let us know how her trip went and to call when she returned.

She promised, and we walked her out.

A couple of weeks went by when I got a call from her, asking to come see me.

I was excited to have her come in so we set the time for later that same day.

When she came in, she was extremely excited and looked healthy and strong. She was not the masked, pasty-complexioned, desperately weak woman dragging around an oxygen bottle, but rather a vital young mother with a bright smile and an infectious laugh.

"Well, tell me all about it. It's obvious that something happened. You look great!" I said.

"Gee thanks!" she smiled. "I feel awesome, but the doctors in Denver are mad at me and my doctor here in Iowa."

"What happened?" I asked, thinking that she had the wrong date or was late and missed the appointment. But she just looked too good for something like that to have happened, I thought.

"Well, when I got there I had my portable oxygen bottle they gave me here," she explained. "But I wasn't using it because I didn't need it. In fact, I realized I wasn't even using my oxygen when I left the church until I got home. At first I just thought I had forgotten it at the church.

"As soon as the nurse met me in Denver, she asked what I was doing there. I told her that I had an appointment for the lung transplant and she asked, 'Why?' I told her what the doctors here told me and she looked on the schedule and said, 'Well, your name's on the schedule.'"

She continued by saying, "The surgeon and his team met me and they listened to my heart, took blood, took X-rays of my lungs and left me sitting in the examining room for over an hour.

"When they came back in, the doctor's first words were, 'You seem to be absolutely fine. Is this some sort of joke?'

"I could tell he was angry, so I began to tear up. But I was afraid to cry. Then he said, 'Tell me your story.'

"I didn't know what to say, so I just told him about talking with you and coming to church to get the financial help I needed and then I got on the plane."

She continued, "They asked me when I noticed that I didn't need the oxygen and it dawned on me that I hadn't used it at all since I left the church."

I asked her, "Do you remember being prayed for when you were here?"

Her eyes blinked and she said, "No. Did someone pray for me?"

I couldn't believe my ears. I recounted to her what I witnessed during her visit. I told her, "I prayed for you but the Lord only led me to say two words."

She asked, "What did you say?"

"New lungs," I said.

"Well, that's what I got. The doctor in Denver told me I have the lungs of a teenager," she said.

"That's why they were upset with me — for taking up their time. But how did I know? I just knew I felt better and I didn't want to miss my appointment. I had been waiting for that transplant for months."

I was blown away that she didn't remember anything that happened that fateful day, except that she came to church, walked in, talked to me, got her money and left.

She couldn't believe it when I told her she slid down the wall and sat motionless on the floor during the entire service.

God obviously put her under divine anesthetic and gave her a new set of lungs while all we saw was a sick woman sitting on the floor.

God even took the worry out of us and made it an awesome service.

Her family became a part of our church and she then lived the very normal life of a young mother.

It has been several years since I have talked to her, but I keep up with her and her kids on Facebook.

Today she is alive and well, thanks to the Acts of Holy Spirit through a regular guy.

Chapter 17
Miracle In Houston

*I*n October of 2010 I received a call from my father and he said, "Larry, I'm sorry but I've got bad news."

My immediate thought was that my mother had been hurt or maybe even passed away as she was 87 at this time. I could tell that whatever it was, it was certainly upsetting my dad who is usually pretty calm.

"Steve is not doing very well and they are going to operate on him this coming Friday!"

"Operate on what?" I asked

"Well, you know all that pain he has been having in his abdomen lately? They just found out it's his pancreas and they think it is either dead or is cancerous. Whatever it is, they said it isn't good and that we need to get there if we want to see him…" then he choked up and I could tell he was crying.

"...If we want to see him before they operate," he spit out.

"Mom and I are going right away. We will be leaving tomorrow and we just wanted you to know what was going on."

Steve is my youngest brother. At that time he was around 58 or 59. He lives in a waterfront town close to Houston, Texas – about an 18-hour drive from my home in Iowa.

At that particular time my parents lived in southwestern Kansas, a good 10-hour drive from my home.

I got off the phone rather dazed and suddenly the gravity of the situation sank in and I found myself in tears at the thought of losing my little brother.

"Lord, what do you want me to do?" I asked.

Very clearly and quickly the answer came "Go pray for Steve and see to it your parents arrive safely."

The Lord's emphasis was, "Pray."

I thought I could pray from right where I was but then the thought of my aged parents traveling that far under fear and stress seemed almost cruel to me.

I had no choice, it was Tuesday afternoon and I needed to drive to southwest Kansas, pick them up and get them to Houston by operation time the coming Friday.

That's 48 hours to drive 28 hours after I made arrangements to be gone several days.

Making my arrangements to be gone was no small feat. I had several appointments to reschedule and others depending upon me at the time.

I called my other brother who only lives a few miles from me and told him what was going on.

He had already heard from the folks and definitely wanted to go. So he said he would meet me in the morning at my house.

I called my dad again and told him to sit tight and we would be there to pick him up as soon as we could get there on Wednesday.

I finished making my arrangements to be gone for who knows how long, fueled up the car, packed a few things and was ready to go by one o'clock Wednesday morning.

We left just after sun-up and drove hard to my parent's home, arriving there by two that afternoon.

Mom and Dad were ready to go.

They had their bags at the door and started moving them toward the car as soon as we arrived.

We took 30 minutes to take a little break, down a soda, drain off the liquid we drank during the past two hours of driving and we were back on the road again.

It was a long, quiet drive, with everyone expecting the worse and fearful of talking about the possibilities.

It was a miserable, arduous drive along the unending road ahead, aggravated by the fatigue from driving since sun-up.

My GPS instructions didn't line up with how my parents remembered going the last time they drove themselves. So there was a continuous undercurrent of feeling, "If we get there late it's because you got us lost."

Finally I couldn't keep my eyes open a minute longer and just inside Oklahoma the lure of a motel's flashing vacancy sign pulled me right in to the office door.

As soon as I got inside my room I slid into one of the beds and was out immediately for the entire night.

A good night's sleep was a gift from God. Everybody was in better spirits and after a quick breakfast we hit the road again.

It was early Thursday morning and Steve's operation was scheduled less than 24 hours hence and we had a good 10 hours of driving remaining.

Dallas traffic was horrible and as we slowly made it through with the morning commuters the thought of being late for Steve's operation was constantly on our mind.

My brother Mike and I both kept encouraging Mom and Dad that this was only

Thursday and the operation wasn't until early the next morning.

Finally, we hit the open road again as we left the Dallas traffic behind us, and sped our way southeast toward Houston.

We finally got there late Thursday evening and thanked God for my kind and helpful little lady friend in the GPS as she guided us right up to Steve's driveway.

I was never so glad to see his family.

We were all bone weary and needed some well-deserved rest.

Steve's family had received an update from the hospital just before we arrived. The operation was at seven o'clock the next morning and Steve needed to be there by five.

They assured me that I would have no problem finding the hospital once I entered the address in my GPS. However, they said we needed to leave by 5 a.m. to beat the traffic; so off to bed we went.

Four o'clock comes early when you don't get to bed before midnight the night before.

What was I thinking – staying up talking past midnight?

Before long we were in the car once again, heading to downtown Houston trying to beat the rush hour traffic. If we did beat the rush hour it was news to me – thank God for modern tech, the GPS unit.

I got my ticket from the valet parking attendant and we rushed toward the elevators.

As we stepped off the elevator on our floor the only nurses' station I could see was all the way down the hall; quite a distance for my parents to walk and keep up with me.

I knew I had to pray for Steve before he went into surgery and it was just a few minutes before seven, the time surgery was scheduled to begin.

I had no clue where to go so I asked Mike to stay with my parents while I sprinted to the nearest nurses' station. As I slid up to the desk I heard someone say, "What's your date of birth, Steven?"

The attending aid was checking the information on Steve's wrist band, comparing the information to the orders on his clipboard.

I said, "Excuse me, sir! I need to pray with this man. He is my brother."

He responded, "Okay, but you must hurry because they are waiting for him in surgery."

I remember what I prayed like it was just yesterday.

"Our Heavenly Father, thank You for getting us here on time. Lord, please grant my brother peace through this ordeal and give the surgeons, nurses and attending physicians the peace and wisdom that go beyond their earthly knowledge.

"Help them see the invisible, Lord. Guide their minds and their hands, and grant them your wisdom. In Jesus' Name, Amen"

L. F. Low

The "amen" came as the attendant began pushing the gurney toward the double steel doors dividing the surgery room from the outside hallway.

I took a deep breath as I said, "I love you, Steve," and through the steel doors they went.

I was so thankful that I made it on time.

Now I just wanted to find the waiting room and sit down with my parents, my other brother and Steve's wife and kids.

The operation was to take up to six hours.

The plan was to disconnect the small intestine from the dead end of the pancreas, take the dead part of his pancreas (about one third), remove it and reconnect the small intestine to the part that was alive.

After reading all the magazines in the family waiting room, drowning myself on sodas, pacing the floor trying to pass the time away and praying continuously, the door opened up and the surgeon and two nurses came in – not a good sign.

Steve's wife jumped to her feet and called the surgeon by name and introduced him to the rest of us. He was very cordial but didn't seem very pleased, so we naturally sensed that something must be amiss.

It had been four hours since Steve was taken into surgery and a nurse from the surgery room had earlier reported that he was under the anesthetic and the doctor had him open and all was going as planned.

However, standing in front of us now was the lead surgeon and his first words were, "I'm afraid we have a problem."

He continued with, "It has taken us all this time just to open him up and prepare for the dissection of the pancreas.

"As we prepared and the surgical team took a good look at Steve's pancreas, we noticed a strange phenomenon; there is a large artery that has attached itself to Steve's pancreas and we are afraid that in trying to separate it from the pancreas it might be cut.

"This would've caused much bleeding and further damage to the pancreas or, worse yet, we may have weakened the wall of the artery that may have started bleeding internally and Steve could have conceivably bled to death before it could be detected."

Everyone looked dazed as the doctor said, "So we have decided to do nothing. Right now the surgical team is putting him back together. He'll be in recovery within the hour."

Steve's wife came unglued.

"What do you mean you have decided to do *nothing*?" she cried. "Isn't there something you can do? You can't just quit on him! You said he could not live without a pancreas."

The doctor tried to console her and my father asked, "Can't you just cut away the part of the pancreas that has died while not touching the artery on the good part?"

As my mother and a nurse tended to Steve's wife, the doctor went on to explain.

"The problem is that the artery is attached to the part that is alive and if we damage that part Steve has no chance at all.

"The pancreas is the most unforgiving gland in the human body," he continued. "And there is just nothing we can do in this case. Believe me, we have all thought and planned and prayed and there is just no room for us to do anything."

He concluded his time with us with, "I am very sorry, but there is just nothing we can do." And he left the room leaving us all rather stunned, and visibly shaken.

Suddenly it came to me and I jumped to my feet, almost excited, and said, "Hold on everybody! The Lord brought us over 1000 miles and I knew He wanted us here to pray. We made it! We prayed! Now let's watch God do what He wants to do!"

I had become the family cheerleader.

"Come on, I'm not giving up on Steve, or God! And neither can you! Now let's thank God for the healing and Steve's recovery! Come on, let's pray!"

I grabbed the hand of the closest one to me as the others looked on sheepishly and began reaching out to take the hand of the one next to them.

"Lord Jesus, we know You can do the impossible. Lord, I know that when the doctors say there is nothing they can do, that should be good news to us who believe. But right now it hurts because we all love Steve and we are very concerned for his life.

"Lord, you didn't send us over 1000 miles to come prepare for a funeral! So, Lord, I am expecting You to heal Steve and bring him through the recovery part quickly and completely. Amen!"

We waited for another couple of hours until a nurse came to get Steve's wife and explain to the rest of us that we could not go in until tomorrow.

As Steve's wife went in to be with Steve, the rest of us started for the car.

"Anybody hungry?" I asked.

That evening was rather miserable from the standpoint of trying to help Steve's kids and wife see the silver lining.

I kept telling them, "God didn't send us here to plan a funeral. We can't give up on God. He has a plan."

I will admit, however, that I wondered in the back of my mind if I had heard from God or if my emotions and my natural protective instincts for my parents had taken over.

When Steve's wife came home from the hospital she said he was resting peacefully in the Intensive Care Unit.

Knowing we had to leave early in the morning because I needed to be home

Monday morning, I asked her if I could visit him first thing in the morning as we left town.

She wasn't sure so she called the hospital and talked to the ICU nurse on duty and mentioned we had to leave so could we visit him for a few minutes in the morning and they said we could.

Early Saturday morning we made it to the ICU and the nurse directed us to Steve's bed.

He was awake and surprisingly alert.

I asked him how he felt and he motioned to his belly area and said in his Texas drawl, "It feeeels like I been cut open."

I asked him if his deep pain he had been experiencing was still there and he said "Nope. Feeeels like the doc got it."

Before I could catch myself I blurted out, "But they weren't able to do anything."

He said, "Well they musta done something 'cause I sure don't hurt like I did when I came in here."

I wanted to jump and shout, "Hallelujah!" Someone *did* do something.

Holy Spirit healed him.

But instead, I told him we had to leave right then, but I definitely wanted to pray with him before I left.

I don't remember much about what I said, but I do remember thanking the Lord for healing my brother and helping him recuperate quickly.

Steve had been on sick leave several weeks prior to this and hadn't been working, so I remember saying "And Lord, please get him on his feet and back to work quickly."

And at that Steve and I both said an emphatic, "Amen!"

I just knew God had healed him. I just knew it – but it was hard to encourage the others to accept it. I knew, though, deep inside, that Steve would be okay.

A few days later we got a call from Steve. He was out of the hospital and he said he was at home resting, waiting for the doctor's release that would allow him to return to work.

We all encouraged him to not rush it.

Steve said he felt fine and that the serious deep pain was gone.

He said his stitches were bugging him but other than sore abdominal muscles that were cut, and itchy staples, he was feeling fine.

Steve was home for over a month as the doctors examined him and continued to figure out what had taken place. It was as if he never had a problem.

All his tests came back normal.

His pancreas was obviously working.

Just before they released him to go to work, they X-rayed him to locate a stint they placed in his small intestine months before his operation to resolve the dying pancreas issue.

Guess what? They never found it.

L. F. Low

The doctor's explanation was that Steve obviously passed the two inch stainless steel stint even though he never felt anything. He also said that that was highly unlikely, however, him not feeling something.

I have a better explanation – God removed it when He healed his pancreas.

Steve continued working for eight more years and retired a year ago. He currently lives in the same town, in a new house, and works in his woodworking shop; enjoying the good life with his family and friends.

Praise the Lord!

Epilogue

"When did the miracles stop, Pastor Larry?" is the question I get occasionally.

The answer is, "They have *not* stopped!"

I try to live in a constant connection to the Holy Spirit. He did not promise to keep me on the cutting edge of what He is doing on earth for just a few years or until I reached retirement age.

No! He promised to keep me on the cutting edge of life as long as I submit to Him. Excitedly, with sky-high expectations, I submit to Him daily.

Physical space and time does not allow me to share all that the Holy Spirit has done, and continues to do, in our lives. Plus, I have already written much about the steady flow of miracles we witness daily.

For instance, how God rescued me from a life of alcoholism, a life of rage, a life of depression. If that interests you, you can check out my book, The Divine Remedy.

Or how God saved Dixie's and my marriage; He took a marriage that was struggling and taught us how to build a relationship strong enough to last the test of time – over 50 years as of this writing.

If the topic of marriage and relationship renewal or marriage preparation interests you, please check out our book, Made In Heaven.

My wife and I co-authored that book because of the hundreds of hurting, failing marriages we have personally helped restore by the same principles God used to restore us to each other and back to Him.

Room does not allow me to share the many day- to-day miracles of building our new church building; everything from raising the financing, buying the land and growing a church out of nothing in a corn field.

Or the miracles that occurred in our church as we worshiped Him; like the young woman who had no inner right ear, but during worship one Sunday morning she heard a pop in the right ear and has heard out of it perfectly ever since.

Currently we serve Him by serving Teen Challenge of the Midlands in Colfax, Iowa.

We are privileged daily to participate with Holy Spirit as He sets men and women free from emotional pain and mental illness that the best medical minds in the world say can never be healed.

All who come to us are in total bondage to drugs, illegal or prescription, their doctors and rehab centers say they cannot live without them – but daily, the Holy Spirit proves them wrong beyond all doubt.

We are watching God free men and women from Tourette's syndrome, Post Traumatic Stress Disorder, Asperger's Syndrome, panic attacks, schizophrenia, bipolar depression, anger and rage, feelings of worthlessness, abandonment, rejection, fear, insignificance and inadequacy – on a *daily* basis.

The list goes on and on.

* * *

Well, okay! One more quickie.

Several years ago my wife and I were guest ministers at a church where we were teaching people how to find perfect inner peace. Many emotionally hurting people were there in hopes of being healed, invited by the members of that church.

After ministering to the congregation, we began meeting those who came to be healed in private until the evening service.

We were almost done when in walked a man helping his wife through the door. She used a walker and it was obvious that she was in a great deal of pain.

The husband explained that his wife was his age, 38 years old, even though she moved like a woman 50 years older than that.

He reported that he had to help her get dressed and take care of herself and she was getting worse and worse as time passed.

He said doctors could find nothing wrong with her and the pain must be fibromyalgia.

I asked the Lord to show her the reason she was in such pain and unable to move and He showed her a memory of when she was two years old. (See my book, Your Pain Is Showing, on this subject).

She was at the bottom of a long staircase where she had just fallen or was pushed down the stairs by her mother. She said, "I always just feel like it would have been better for me to have been born dead."

I asked her to report what the Lord had to say about that, and after she told us what she sensed the Lord saying there were no other memories.

We sat and talked for about 20 more minutes when she said, "You know, I am beginning to feel better just being here."

I asked her to get up and move around a bit. She got straight up without help and bent over to tie her shoe. Her husband was beside himself as he exclaimed, "She hasn't done that in months!"

She got up, hugged my wife and me and walked out of the room without her walker. I asked her if she wanted it and she said without hesitation, "Nope! I don't plan on needing that thing ever again!" as she sauntered into the sanctuary for the evening service.

The Holy Spirit strikes again! Another one healed by the power of God!

I haven't addressed the miracles the Holy Spirit has done in my children's life and how God saved the life of my youngest daughter and her children.

Nor have I related about the day my middle daughter hit a little boy with her van and how she was visited by an angel who told her what to say; she spoke it as she was praying for the boy and he not only lived but never sustained anything worse than a little bruise.

Those are their stories and maybe they will write about them themselves one day.

No, the miracles have not stopped. They continue as long as we trust Him and put ourselves in a place where, if He doesn't move, we fail.

We never fail because He never fails!

Our ministry is seeing salvations daily – which are the greatest miracle of all.

I have learned to live my life in the reality of eternity. This means that, because I am a spirit man, I will never die – and what I am doing today is my current assignment.

Tomorrow may be different; if the Holy Spirit informs me of any change in assignment, then – absolutely, without question – I will resolutely follow Him.

Until then I will keep walking with Him, enjoying the Holy Spirit's friendship and anticipating His next move until we all meet in our Heavenly abode.

Made in the USA
Lexington, KY
27 June 2017